AN ALBUM OF
CIVIL WAR BATTLE ART

APPLEWOOD BOOKS
CAMBRIDGE
1988

ISBN: 1-55709-111-0

CIVIL WAR BATTLE ART

INTRODUCTION

INTRODUCTION

APART from the recurrent Indian wars, which concerned only the outermost layer of the population, and the brief, triumphant interlude of the Mexican War, the United States had enjoyed nearly half a century of peace. But now the question became increasingly insistent whether the United States, in any real and national sense, existed. The grand problem of Slavery had always been troublesome in a nation that had established itself upon Jefferson's Declaration of Independence, and most of the Southern Founders had looked upon it as an evil that had to be presently endured, but ought to be progressively lessened and eventually done away with. After Whitney's cotton gin had led the South to change its mind on the subject, and brought it into an inconvenient dependence on a single staple, there did exist an irrepressible conflict, and the only question was whether statesmanship could prevent its taking a violent and military form. The Slavery issue was compromised in 1820 and again in 1850, but there was no easing of tension during the fifties. In 1854 a too clever presidential aspirant from Illinois destroyed the second compromise by his Kansas-Nebraska Act, and the North, aroused at last, became politically aggressive. Six years later the Democratic Party split, and "Black Republicans," led by an almost unknown attorney from Springfield, Ill., carried the national elections. Almost at once the fiery State of South Carolina met in convention and seceded from the Union, and the rest of the Southern States followed at intervals, while a bewildered President looked helplessly on at the dissolution of the Union he was sworn to protect.

There were to be four long and terrible years of a brothers' war. The South had a naturally military population and superior generalship, especially that of Robert E. Lee, one of the tactical geniuses of history. The Union, in army and administration alike, fumbled and stumbled. But, apart from the possibility of overwhelming defeat in battle, everything was on the side of the Union: numbers, industrial and food resources, transportation, sea power and communication with the rest of the world. After disasters such as First and Second Bull Run, Fredericksburg, and Chancellorsville, and disappointments and lost opportunities without number, the tide began to turn in July 1863. Meade inflicted a bloody check upon Lee at Gettysburg, and Grant captured the stronghold of Vicksburg on the Mississippi. Grant now came East, and, while directing a coherent forward movement of all the Federal armies, himself engaged Lee in mid-Virginia. The Confederacy struggled with a bravery and tenacity never surpassed on this planet, but its road lay steadily downhill to Appomatox.

In this section we present the greatest number of our plates from any single hand—16 pencil-and-wash drawings by ALFRED R.

WAUD. When Pvt. Lincoln Kirstein was making his survey of materials for the Battle Art Exhibitions, it at once became apparent to him, and has since been fairly obvious to everyone else concerned, that Alfred Waud is one of the most important illustrators of American history that we have, and that in its collection of his drawings the Library of Congress has a great and a singularly neglected treasure. But who has ever heard of Alfred R. Waud?—we do not even know his middle name. There are, we think, several reasons for his undeserved but almost complete obscurity. In the first place, Alfred Waud's drawings were made for publication in *Harper's Weekly,* in the course of which they were turned into wood engravings—commercial "quickies"—and lost, as a rule, every atom of their individuality and artistic value. Even the superior reproductions in *Battles and Leaders of the Civil War* retain almost nothing of the quality of the originals. In the second, Waud's style was not one likely to impress his contemporaries: instead of the mid-Victorian heavy finish, he employed a quick, light touch, an impressionism and even a shorthand which are thoroughly modern and are characteristic of drawings made 50 years later. We are not claiming, of course, that Waud's drawings are comparable to Raphael's or Michelangelo's; but we are certain that, considering their purpose and the conditions under which they were made, they are very, very good

by any standards. Finally, the drawings came to the Library just after the First World War, and the twenties had their attentions focussed on a different sphere of art. In 1937, however, Prof. J. G. Randall used some of them as illustrations in that nonpareil among our historical textbooks, *The Civil War and Reconstruction;* although he seems to have preferred Forbes.

The Alfred Waud drawings are a part of the J. Pierpont Morgan Collection, presented to the Library of Congress by the financier and connoisseur in 1918. The Collection also includes drawings by Alfred's brother, WILLIAM WAUD, likewise an able artist if less gifted than his brother, and by the much better known EDWIN FORBES. We reproduce three drawings by William Waud, two of which illustrate his characteristic and skillful use of wash; and two drawings (one a double plate) and one etching by Forbes. In spite of their greater reputation, Forbes' pencil drawings will not stand comparison with the Wauds'; in that light they appear as heavy, stiff, lifeless, and uninspired. Nevertheless, he remains an important illustrator, and occasionally rose above himself, as in Plate 99.

At present we know little about Alfred Waud's life and career, although it is a subject which the Library proposes to investigate further. *Appleton's Annual Cyclopedia* for 1891 carried an obituary from which we learn that he was an Englishman, born in London in 1828, and that he received his artistic education there. Coming to New York in 1858, he exhibited at the National Academy of Design, but made his living as an illustrator of periodicals and books. After the war broke out came the great opportunity of his life, as "special artist" or pictorial correspondent for *Harper's Weekly.* We have a letter (July 5, 1862) written by him soon after the Peninsular Campaign. He has barely recovered from a "billious remittent fever—brought on by exposure to the damned climate in the cussed swamps," but outlines the dreadful hardships of the Seven Days' Battles: "Only think of it, seven days almost without food or sleep, night and day being attacked by overwhelming masses of infuriated rebels, thundering at us from all sides . . ." From this letter as well as various contributions to *Harper's* it is clear that he could express himself in words as well as in pictures. He seems to have formed a particular friendship with the able General Gouverneur K. Warren, who 15 years later called for his help in clearing up the question of Warren's supersession at Five Forks. General Patrick complimented him for having never incorporated in his sketches any information which could be of service to the enemy. After the war Gen. O. O. Howard recommended Waud to the agents of the Freedman's Bureau as a man whom he had found, when he was in command of the Army of the Tennessee, "to be a genial, educated gentleman," and one worthy of all confidence. In 1868 Charles

Parsons of Harper's Art Department recommended him to all and sundry as a gentleman competent to execute book or other illustration. In the eighties Alfred Waud contributed his sketches to illustrate the series of articles in the *Century* which became *Battles and Leaders of the Civil War,* but he was given no preëminence among the numerous artists who contributed to that unique work. In 1891, according to the obituary already quoted, he "was making an extended sketching tour of the battlefields in the South" when he died, on April 6, at Marietta, Ga.

Of William Waud we can say even less. We have a letter (October 3, 1864) from him to Alfred, showing that he and his brother were on the most affectionate terms. In the spring of 1862 he went to cover Butler's expedition to New Orleans for *Frank Leslie's Illustrated Newspaper,* which printed a picture of him, complete with bowler hat, sketching in the foretop of one of Farragut's big ships. Had **we** found it in time, we should have reproduced it here. He returned to sketch for *Leslie's* the Peninsular Campaign which his brother was covering for *Harper's* but was disabled by sunstroke and fever. In 1864, by which time he had joined his brother on the staff of *Harper's,* he lost his clothes, blankets and sketchbook in a Confederate raid, and Alfred sent him fresh drawing materials.

Louis J. M. Daguerre announced his epoch-making discovery in January 1839, and within a few years it had spread all through the Western world, and was making the fortunes of those sagacious individuals who had early mastered its technique. A few daguerreotypes were made during the Mexican War, probably by a Mexican practitioner. One of these dim but fascinating relics is reproduced on page 225 of Robert Taft's *Photography and the American Scene*. In Europe, there was considerable photography of the Crimean War (1855), but the first American war to be extensively recorded by the camera was the Civil War. That it was so was almost entirely the work of one man, MATHEW B. BRADY (c. 1823–96), "the most prominent name in the whole history of American photography." Brady entered upon his Civil War work in the spirit of a sacred duty; there was no material reason why he should have sought the dust and danger of the battlefield. He was the most fashionable and prosperous photographer in New York City, or in the country, and generals, admirals, and heroes would have come to sit for him either there or at his Washington gallery. But, as he said, "I felt that I had to go. A spirit in my feet said 'go' and I went."

To Bull Run he went in 1861, getting as far as Blackburne's Ford, and there, as the *American Journal of Photography* reported in its August number, with the rest of our Grand Army he was completely routed. He managed to salvage his wagons of equipment, but in a battered condition. Thereafter he organized the business of photographing the war on a large scale; since he could not be everywhere himself he hired a staff of photographers, at times employing as many as 20 men, and made a total investment of well over $100,000. Although at his Washington headquarters he was sufficiently busy in directing his field workers as well as his two galleries, he went to the battlefield when he got wind of important operations: he came under fire at Fredericksburg in 1862 and Petersburg in 1864, and he reached Antietam and Gettysburg before there had been time to bury the dead. He and his staff are thought to have taken more than 3,500 negatives, a tremendous documentation of the utmost variety, every possible kind of scene, in fact, where there was not actual motion—to photograph bodies in motion was a task beyond the slow cameras of Brady's day.

It is sad to have to record that Brady was financially ruined by his creation of what should have been, and now is, regarded as a national heritage. The Government eventually paid him $25,000 for a part of his collection of negatives, too late to break his fall into bankruptcy; the other part had to be disposed of in payment of a debt for photographic supplies. Brady's last years were spent most undeservedly in labor, illness, and poverty. The part of his collection purchased by the Government is now in the National Archives, while the other part, long in private hands, has very recently been acquired by the Library of Congress. This part also includes the Alexander Gardner Collection of negatives, purchased and incorporated with it at a later date. If we have included relatively few Civil War photographs, it is not because we underrate their documentary value; it is merely that many of them are not precisely art, and that the whole *corpus* has been effectively exploited in such works as the 10-volume *Photographic History of the Civil War,* edited by Francis T. Miller (New York, 1911).

THE ALBUM

1861. The backwoods lawyer took his oath as Chief Executive of the United States. He said in his inaugural address: "The power confided to me will be used to hold, occupy and possess the the property and places belonging to the government . . . but beyond what may be necessary for these objects, there will be . . . no using of force . . ."

On April 12 the irrepressible conflict broke out. Fort Sumter stood in the middle of the entrance to Charleston Harbor. Fort Johnson, opposing her, had been already seized by the authorities of the first secession State, South Carolina. The surrender of Sumter had been demanded and refused. The Confederate States of America had adopted a constitution. President Lincoln was readying an expedition from New York for the relief of Fort Sumter. On April 11 General Beauregard demanded the evacuation of the fort, and Maj. Robert Anderson, in command of the skeleton garrison of 65 men, refused. At 4:30 the next morning Forts Johnson and Moultrie and the batteries on Morris and Sullivan's Islands opened fire.

According to Capt. (later General) Abner Doubleday, one of Anderson's officers and author of the article, "From Moultrie to Sumter," in *Battles and Leaders of the Civil War*, "We have not been in the habit of regarding the signal shell fired from Fort Johnson as the first gun of the conflict, although it was undoubtedly aimed at Fort Sumter. Edmund Ruffin of Virginia is usually credited with opening the attack by firing the first gun from the iron-clad battery on Morris Island. The ball from that gun struck the wall of the magazine where I was lying, penetrated the masonry, and burst very near my head."

The bombardment lasted through 40 hours, without casualties but with great damage by fire to the inflammable structures within the fort. By evening of the 13th Sumter's ammunition was nearly exhausted. At seven o'clock terms of surrender were agreed upon. Major Anderson's handful of Union troops marched out the ruined walls next day, saluting the Stars and Stripes with a volley of 50 guns.

PAGE 18: *Negroes mounting Cannon in the works for the attack on Ft. Sumter 1861–Morris Island.*

March, 1861.
by W. Waud.
Wash drawing.
On green tinted paper.
9 1/4 x 13 inches.

PAGE 19: *Interior of Fort Sumter. During the Bombardment, April 12, 1861.*

Published by Currier & Ives.
Lithograph, colored by hand.
8 3/8 x 11 3/4 inches.

INTERIOR OF FORT SUMTER.
DURING THE BOMBARDMENT, APRIL 12TH 1861

"Winfield Scott, General-in-chief of the U. S. Army, infirm in body but robust in mind, advised the President that at least 300,000 men, a general of Wolfe's capacity, and two or three years' time would be required to conquer even the lower South" (Morison & Commager). But that was not the attitude of the man in the street or of the Administration. Lincoln's proclamation of April 15, 1861, called for only 75000 volunteers, for three months, to reinforce a regular army which during the months of secession between December 1860 and March 4, 1861 had shrunk from 16,367 officers and men to 13,024. Most disastrous of all, of the 900-odd West Point officers in the service, 269 had resigned and 26 had been dismissed to join the Confederacy. One hundred and eighty-two officers who held during the war the rank of brigadier general or higher, were furnished to the South from the United States Army.

The Confederacy had at its head a trained soldier, Jefferson Davis. A month before Fort Sumter he had called for 100,000 12-month volunteers. Southerners were horsemen, used to handling weapons, and inspired by what they felt to be the cause of freedom. They did not care for discipline, and their social system provided too many officers, but for leaders they had such men as Beauregard, the two Johnstons, Thomas J. Jackson, the two Hills, and J. E. B. Stuart. Robert E. Lee had refused the offer of supreme field command made him by his former chief, Scott, and had gone with the State of Virginia to which he felt the higher allegiance.

At Lincoln's call the State militia and the volunteers tumbled over themselves in patriotic enthusiasm and Zouave uniforms. Officers were appointed by the State governors, or elected by the untrained recruits themselves. Able young officers of the regular army, men like Philip Sheridan, were not permitted to leave their own units and provide a stiffening in the regiments of the heterogeneous new masses—farmer boys, factory workers and city clerks, many of whom had never held a gun in their hands. McClellan, Grant, Sheridan, many other former West Pointers, were returning obscurely to the army from civil life. In short, the South had several months' head start, and Gen. Winfield Scott, as Alfred Waud has drawn him behind his council table, was perfectly cognizant of the fact. Shown with the septuagenarian general are three members of his staff, Cols. George Washington Cullum, who later compiled the register of West Point graduates, Schuyler Hamilton, and Henry Van Rensselaer.

Naval affairs, on the other hand, were weighted on the Union side. The Confederacy came into the war with no navy and few important seaports. The resourcefulness of the naval officers who "went South" produced a few ships, but Federal superiority at sea was as nearly absolute throughout the war as at the beginning.

The few Confederate raiders raised Northern insurance rates skyhigh, and British sympathy for the South and competition for the carrying trade, while it nearly ruined the U. S. merchant marine, had little military effect.

In mid-March, 1861 the U. S. Navy had a total of 90 ships, of which only 42 were in commission, and of these only 12 in the Home Squadron. Soon after the inauguration orders went to 15 vessels, most of the steam ships of the fleet, to return from the foreign stations where they were scattered—report said by the evil intent of the late Secretary of the Navy, Isaac Toucey—and repairs and new construction began in the shipyards. Waud's charming sketch of the Washington Navy Yard shows this renewed activity—chimneys smoking, small boats going to and fro, a large ship having its mast re-stepped, and a new hull nearing completion in the totally closed way.

PAGE 22: *General Scott and his Staff: Gen. Winfield Scott, Colonel Van Rensselaer, Lieutenant Colonel Cullom, Lieutenant Colonel Hamilton*

Pencil and wash drawing by A.R. Waud.
Undated.
10 x 14 1/2 inches.

PAGE 23: *Washington Navy Yard 1861*

Drawing by A.R. Waud.
5 3/4 x 9 inches.

Washington Navy Yard 186

On the 19th and 27th of April President Lincoln issued two proclamations which declared the coast of the new Confederacy under blockade, from Washington down the Potomac, through the Chesapeake Bay to the sea, south on the Atlantic and West on the Gulf, to that same extreme tip of Texas where Matthew Calbraith Perry's squadron had rested 14 years before. It was time; President Davis had authorized privateering, and the daring sea raiders were soon to be at work. Off the Mississippi river, out of Charleston, out of Hatteras Inlet the *Calhoun,* the *Jefferson Davis,* the North Carolina ships *Winslow, Raleigh,* and *Beaufort* operated with increasing success, and increasing alarm among Northern shipowners.

At Hatteras Inlet on Pamlico Sound there stood two small forts, Clark and Hatteras, which protected the comings and goings of the privateers and blockade runners bearing supplies to the army of Virginia. On August 27, 1861, an expedition appeared before the inlet, five steamers and an army tug, the *Fanny,* led by the 40-gun *Minnesota,* from which flew the pennant of Flag Officer S. H. Stringham. [This title was replaced in 1862 by the rank of Rear Admiral.] Land forces came too, in several transports, 860 men under Benjamin F. Butler of Massachusetts. Part of Butler's troops were landed, as Waud's drawing shows, in the surf, under cover of the lighter vessels. As in most landings, there were difficulties; the heavy iron surfboats stuck on the beach, and two flatboats hit rocks. Three hundred and fifteen troops, some of them marines, reached the shore dripping, their provisions lost, and their ammunition soaked. Their activity was limited to a parade down the beach, where they hoisted the flag over Fort Clark, the smaller Confederate work, which had been abandoned at the first round from the Minnesota's big guns. Fort Hatteras held out till midmorning of the 29th, then ran up a white flag. The chief Confederate waterway north of Charleston was controlled by the Union, and the success was comforting a month after disastrous Bull Run. Butler, strictly a political general, acquired a reputation considerably in excess of his actual abilities.

Minnesota   Cumberland Wabash   Susquehanna   Fort Clark   Fort Hatteras

Harriet Lane

Capture of the Forts at Hatteras Inlet — First Day. Flotilla firing and Troops landing thro' the Surf.

PAGE 27: *The Great Expedition. The Vessels at Anchor at Hampton Roads, From the Top of the Hygeia Hotel, Old Point Comfort, VA*

E. Sachse & Co. Published by C. Bohn. Lithograph, printed in color. 8 1/2 x 16 3/4 inches.

The Hatteras affair gained for the U. S. Navy control of the northernmost Confederate coast line, but a naval base was needed nearer the main southern ports if an effective blockade was to be maintained. This was acquired by the important and successful Port Royal expedition, which left Hampton Roads on October 29, 1861, under Flag Officer S. F. DuPont, and crossed the bar of Port Royal Sound on November 4. The transports bearing troops had been scattered by a gale, and DuPont attacked with the fleet alone, "wooden ships against heavy land fortifications in narrow waters" (D. W. Knox). In a bold and skilfully conducted bombardment of four and a half hours on November 7, DuPont silenced the guns of Fort Walker, the stronger of the two forts protecting the sound. The Confederates evacuated the position, as well as Fort Beauregard on the opposite point, and Port Royal became an invaluable Union base for the remainder of the war.

Our lithograph shows the assembling of the "Great Expedition" at Hampton Roads. From the "widow's walk" of the stylish health-resort hotel the surface of the sea seems blanketed with sail. They had been begged, borrowed and bought for the purpose; warships, transports and coaling schooners now crowded the Roads. Twenty-five coaling vessels, convoyed by a sloop-of-war, got an advance start on October 28. On the morning of the 29th, 50 vessels steamed out of the harbor, forming a double echelon line outside Cape Henry, and proceeded, under sealed orders, to the south.

The lithograph is from the house of EDWARD SACHSE & Co., Baltimore, which did business from 1857 to 1866. They made many good views, mainly of scenes in the South, Baltimore, and Washington. During the war they specialized in military and naval prints, of which Worrel's "Merrimac and Monitor" is noteworthy. Sachse had already, before the war, drawn "Fort Monroe, Old Point Comfort, and Hygeia Hotel, Va." possibly at the instigation of the proprietors of the hotel, to whom he does the favor of advertising their resort in connection with the great naval display.

FORTRESS MONROE   RIP RAPS.

Ent.accord. to an Act of Congress in the year 1851 by C.Bohn in the Clerks Office of the Dist.of Columbia.

Published by C.Bohn, Washington D.C.

THE GREAT EXPEDITION._THE VESSELS AT ANCHOR AT HAMPTON ROADS,
FROM THE TOP OF THE HYGEIA HOTEL, OLD POINT COMFORT, VA.

The beautiful slope-of-war, U. S. S. *Cumberland*, 24 guns, Lt. G. U. Morris acting in command, sank below the waters of Hampton Roads, March 8, 1862, her colors flying and her splendid crew steady and defiant, at their guns to the last. Her sister ship, the *Congress*, greatly damaged and her commander killed, hauled down her flag. The other Union vessels huddled in panic off Fortress Monroe to the eastward, as the Confederate ironclad *Virginia* steamed back into the Elizabeth River and Norfolk Harbor. A shock of alarm ran through the North—was this new weapon invincible? Would our cities be shelled, our commerce destroyed, our coast blockaded, our defeat insured? "To all these terrible questions the triumphant *Virginia* seemed to answer 'yes,' " and the North was stunned.

But on the next day the answer was "no"! At nine o'clock in the evening of that terrible Saturday, the tug *Seth Low* out of New York steamed into Hampton Roads towing a singular contraption, John Ericsson's new-fangled turret ship, *Monitor*, mounting exactly two 11-inch smooth-bores. However unimpressive she may have appeared, there was no choice but to try her out, and when the *Virginia* made her anticipated appearance at eight o'clock on Sunday morning, the little *Monitor* took her on. The two vessels exchanged a furious cannonade without inflicting the least damage on each other, until the *Virginia* gave up and returned to Norfolk. "No transition from an old to a new era of naval combat was ever more clearly marked for public understanding" (D. W. Knox).

The novelty was properly in the clash of the two indestructible bodies, not in the idea of armored vessels. These had been the subject of experiment from antiquity, and of serious effort in Europe and the United States since the forties. The French had launched the iron-clad *Gloire* in 1859 and were building a seagoing armored fleet; the British were following suit. Union and Confederate naval architects since the beginning of the war had been rushing designs for ironclads, and the Confederates had won. Says James Phinney Baxter of the *Cumberland*:

"Of the five great naval revolutions of the nineteenth century—steam, shell guns, the screw propeller, rifled ordnance, and armor—one only had influenced her design or equipment; nothing but her heavy battery of 9-inch smooth-bore shell guns would have seemed wholly unfamiliar to the conquerers of the Spanish Armada. But the crude *Virginia,* whose iron prow had just dealt the graceful *Cumberland* her deathblow, embodied all five of those revolutionary features."

In early 1861 the Norfolk Navy Yard had been destroyed to prevent its falling into Confederate hands, and the former U. S. steam frigate *Merrimack,* with engines already condemned as unseaworthy, had been scuttled and burned to the water's edge. The Confederate engineers raised the hull, cut her down almost to the water, and put on her deck a wooden citadel with sloping sides, plated with two thin layers of iron strips. They rechristened her *Virginia*. From 10 openings protruded huge guns—the smoke is belching from them in two prints. On the 9th of March 1862, she was without her wedge-shaped cast-iron ram, torn away by the shock when she sank the *Cumberland* the day before. Her captain, Flag Officer Buchanan, had been sent back wounded to Norfolk, and she faced the *Monitor* under her second in command, Lt. Catesby ap R. Jones. Had he been able to use the ram, the outcome of this day might conceivably have been different, for the tiny "cheesebox on a raft" bore marks on her side where the mutilated *Virginia* had struck a glancing blow.

The *Monitor,* which gave her name to a class of Federal ironclads, was designed for the United States Government by the Swedish engineer, John Ericsson. His plans were submitted on October 4, 1861, and within four hours the contract was being drawn up and the iron plates started through the rolling mill. She consisted quite simply of a hull nearly awash and a revolving gun turret, to the general adoption of which her success gave wide impetus. She had been built in 100 days, but was not ready for sea until March 3. Then steering troubles took her back to New York, and on the second attempt she had to be towed part way south. She reached Hampton Roads in the evening of March 8, and learned from the distressed *Minnesota* of the disaster just over and the crisis ahead. The crews of both ships worked all night to put the little David in condition.

The famous fight of March 9 lasted four hours. The first print, lithographed from Worrel's drawing, shows accurately the positions in the Roads. The large *Minnesota* lay grounded at the right; in the center the two ironclads turned and maneuvred in their history-making conflict. Several times the speedier *Monitor* retreated to shallow water to renew the ammunition supply in her turret, and then the *Minnesota* suffered from the Confederate guns.

The artillery duel, much of it at point-blank range, was strangely futile—the poor-quality cast-iron shot of the *Monitor,* and the shells of the *Virginia,* proved equally ineffective against the other's armor. Finally the *Virginia's* gunners struck the *Monitor's* pilot house and the iron splinters blinded her captain, John L. Worden. He directed the pilot to shallow water, and Jones thought it meant flight. The Confederate captain delivered a last blow at the helpless *Minnesota,* then, fearing the ebbing tide of the Elizabeth River, steered for Norfolk. The hope of the Confederacy lay stalemated in the harbor, while the army of the Union gathered against Norfolk.

Sgt. CHARLES WORREL, whose sketch was made into a wood-engraving for *Harper's*

PAGE 31: *The Naval Engagement between the Merrimac and the Monitor at Hampton Roads on the 9th of March 1862.*

Drawn on the spot by Charles Worret. Lithograph, printed in color.
9 x 16 1/3 inches.

Weekly before it was lithographed by Sachse, was probably from New York or the vicinity. In both pictures his name is wrongly given, as Worret. He was a member of Company G, 20th Regiment of New York Volunteers, the "United Turner Rifles", a two-year regiment recruited in New York in May 1861. Worrel was 42 when he was mustered in, on May 7, and immediately promoted to sergeant. On October 4, 1862, he was commissioned as lieutenant. The service of the regiment was mainly at Fortress Monroe, from which Worrel doubtless watched the engagement of the ironclads. Worrel remained in service at Fort Monroe until December 29, 1863, when he resigned.

1. Sewall's Point Battery 30 Guns _ 2 Craney Island Battery 42 Guns _ 3 Yorktown _ 4 Jamestown _ 5 Monitor _ 6 Merrimac _ 7 Norfolk _ 8 Portsmouth _ 9 Suffolk _ 10 Minnesota _ 11 Pig Point Battery _ 12 Barre Point Battery 13 Burning of the Congress _ 14 The Cumberland's sunk _ 15 Newport News Point & Camp _ 16 St Lawrence _ 17 Rip Raps _ 18 French Man of War.

THE NAVAL ENGAGEMENT BETWEEN THE MERRIMAC AND THE MONITOR AT HAMPTON ROADS

ON THE 9TH OF MARCH 1862.

PAGE 33: *Monitor Grand March*

Composed by E. Mack.
First page of sheet music.
Lithograph, printed in color.
7 x 9 7/8 inches.

The colored lithograph of the ironclads in combat on the front page of E. Mack's triumphant musical composition was printed by THOMAS S. SINCLAIR, an established Philadelphia lithographer. The business which he opened in 1839 continued until 1889, eight years after his own death. He was a Scotsman, from the Orkney Isles, and had learned the art in Edinburgh. In 1848 he was awarded a prize by the Franklin Institute, and again for his chromolithography in 1849 and 1851. He specialized in views of buildings and in large fashion plates, doing the color work for S. A. & A. F. Ward of Philadelphia. Although he was not one of the outstanding men in the trade, his work has a certain distinction and variety, with some feeling for timeliness and journalism.

We show three of Sinclair's lithographs, the present plate, and the two views of Andersonville prison, his most notable Civil War prints

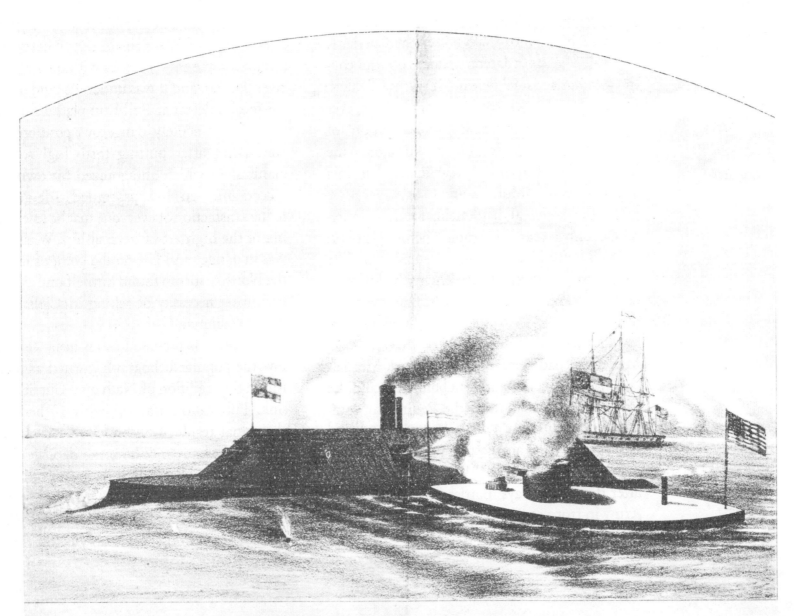

GRAND MARCH,

COMPOSED BY

E. MACK.

LEE & WALKER

PAGE 35: *The Second Battle of Bull Run, Fought Aug. 29th 1862.*

Published by Currier & Ives. Lithograph, colored by hand. Undated. 7 7/8 x 12 3/8 inches.

The Second Battle of Bull Run, or Manasses (29–30 August 1862) was not, as the Currier & Ives print boasts, a Union victory. On the contrary, it was a dismal defeat. "It was the neatest, cleanest bit of work that Lee and Jackson ever performed. The irresistible combination of bold strategy and perfect tactics had undone the Union gains of an entire year in the Virginia theatre of war" (Morison and Commager).

On the identical battlefield, as the caption relates, only a year and a month before (July 21, 1861) Thomas Jackson's brigade had stood like a stone wall, and the Federal Army had broken and fled in disorder from the first major engagement of the war. In the intervening year authorities had shifted in the Army of the Potomac. McDowell had been swiftly removed, McClellan placed in command. Snubbing Lincoln, he had chosen to undertake the Peninsular campaign, and in return had been checked and hampered by the amateur strategy of the President and his Secretary of War, Stanton. Finally, after the Seven Days' Battles, when the Union Army in front of Richmond was pounced on by Lee and Jackson, and driven back to its new base on the James, McClellan was put in a subordinate command. The President called Gen. John Pope from the Western theatre, where he had achieved some easy victories with the help of the river flotillas, and it was under his guidance that the second defeat at Bull Run placed the Union in the most acutely dangerous position of the war. Pope, after putting forth high-sounding manifestoes which antagonized his own army, officers and men alike, proceeded to demonstrate to the satisfaction of everyone that he knew nothing of the high art of generalship. Washington was in danger and Lee on the point of invading the North. Lincoln found himself under the embarrassing necessity of asking McClellan to reassume command.

The print is included as an instance of how low the popular lithograph, treated as journalism in the tradition of Nathaniel Currier, could sink. Publication was evidently rushed before the actual result of Second Bull Run could be adequately known. The scene depicted has no individuality whatever; it is any mass of soldiers driving before them any other mass of soldiers, on a characterless field. Fortunately, Currier and Ives could do considerably better than this in representing battle.

PUBLISHED BY CURRIER & IVES.	152 NASSAU ST. NEW YORK.

THE SECOND BATTLE OF BULL RUN, FOUGHT AUGT 29TH 1862.

Between the "Army of Virginia" under Majr Genl John Pope, and the combined forces of the Rebel Army under Lee, Jackson and others. This terrific battle was fought on the identical battle field of Bull-run, and lasted with great fury from daylight until after dark, when the rebels were driven back, and the Union Army rested in triumph on the field.

Said *Harper's Weekly* on September 27, 1862:

"We publish on page 612 a fine picture of the FIRST VIRGINIA CAVALRY, one of the crack regiments of the rebel service. Mr. Waud writes:

Being detained with the enemy's lines, an opportunity occurred to make a sketch of one of the two crack regiments of the Confederate service. They seemed to be of considerable social standing, that is, most of them F. F. V.'s, so to speak, and not irreverently; for they were not only as a body handsome, athletic men, but generally polite and agreeable in manner. With the exception of the officers, there was little else but homespun among them, light drab-gray or butternut color, the drab predominating; although there were so many varieties of dress, half-citizen, half-military, that they could scarcely be said to have a uniform. Light jackets and trowsers with black facings, and slouched hats, appeared to be (in those cases where the wearer could obtain it) the court costume of the regiment. Their horses were good; in many cases, they told me, they provided their own. Their arms were the United States cavalry sabre, Sharp's carbine, and pistols. Some few of them had old swords of the Revolution, curved, and in broad, heavy scabbards.

"Their carbines, they said, were mostly captured from our own cavalry, for whom they expressed utter contempt—a feeling unfortunately shared by our own army. Finally, they bragged of having their own horses, and, in many cases, of having drawn no pay from the Government, not needing the paltry remuneration of a private. The flag represented in the picture is the battle-flag. White border, red ground, blue cross, and white stars."

The First Virginia Cavalry was part of Gen. Fitzhugh Lee's brigade of five regiments which, with two others, Gen. Wade Hampton's and Gen. B. H. Robertson's brigades, made up the Cavalry Division of Lee's army. The commander of the Division was Maj. Gen. J. E. B. Stuart, *beau sabreur* of the South, who twice, during the peninsular campaign (June 12-15, 1862) and again in October, rode his cavalry around McClellan's entire army. We are told in confirmation of Waud's comment, that during this October raid, when McClellan reported that his cavalry horses were too fatigued to move, Lincoln sarcastically inquired "what the horses of your army have done since the battle of Antietam that fatigues anything?" The command of the regiment itself, according to the *Official Reports,* went through rapid changes. On March 31, 1862, Stuart's report mentions Col. W. E. Jones as leader of the First Virginia Cavalry. On August 6th, he writes to Lee from near Fredericksburg that the enemy had its "cavalry advance guard driven back with loss yesterday by Lt. Col. [James H.] Drake, First Virginia Cavalry." By August 27 the reports mention as leader Lt. Col. L. T. Brien.

In Fredericksburg, the pretty little town on the bank of the Rappahannock, where the ladies refer to the "late unpleasantness," but prefer tales of Washington's mother, they show bullet holes in old walls facing the river. The point out Marye's Heights to the West, and show where the "sunken road" at the base of the hill led to the impregnable stone wall. They name Lee's hill, where the general, a master player of the game, stood musing—"It is well that war is so terrible—we should grow too fond of it." Beneath that stone wall on December 13, 1862, six times Burnside's blue-clad infantry charged with bayonets across the open plain, and six times fell back, the dead piled literally three deep. The casualties decimated the Army of the Potomac in the most useless sacrifice of the Civil War.

Alfred R. Waud did a number of sketches of the Fredericksburg disaster for *Harper's Weekly*. The two plates here reproduced give an excellent idea of how untenderly the process of wood-engraving treated the artist's work. Waud's word-picture of the battle tells the story of the "magnificent defensible position, strong as Sebastopol," against which "our troops were hurled all day,"—French's division, Sturgis's division, Hancock's and Howard's divisions, "each charging more eagerly than its predecessors . . . The sun had set behind the rebel fortifications . . . The rebel fire breaks out with more ferocity than ever. For sweeping across the fields come the divisions of Generals Humphreys and Griffin. Onward, a forlorn hope, they advance—the ground encumbered by the countless bodies of the fallen; knapsacks, blankets, guns, haversacks, canteens, cartridge-boxes, etc., strewed over the plain. Shot, shell, canister, shrapnel, and grape is hurled as they approach. By column of regiments, led by their generals, and without firing a shot, that noble band continues on. General Humphreys, dashing ahead to a small rise in the ground, takes off his hat to cheer on his men. With reckless ardor his men, rapidly closing on the double-quick, answer cheers with cheers. Every member of the General's staff has been dismounted. The brave Humphreys himself has two horses shot under him . . .

"Humphreys' division has never been under fire till this battle. But before that awful hurricane of bullets no heroism can avail. The hillside appears to vomit forth fire, its leven glare flashing through the fast-thickening obscurity seems to pour with redoubled power upon our storming columns, till, being unable to stand up against it longer—although within eighty yards of the wall—the brave remnant, singing in the *abandon* of its courage, marches steadily back to the place where it formed for the charge, leaving its comrades in swathes upon the bloody ground, where, 'stormed at by shot and shell,' they had been cut down, whole ranks at a time, by that terrible fire."

The Army of the Potomac, tremendous, eager, fantastically brave, was at the mercy of the worst leadership of the war. After Pope's removal, "Little Mac," the darling of the troops, rode out to meet the beaten army, and was greeted with wild enthusiasm. Lincoln gave him, verbally, command of forces in the field, and within a week he was marching toward Frederick, where Lee had invaded Maryland. At South Mountain and Antietam, September 16 and 17, 1862, he caught Lee in a cramped spot and won a technical victory, but failed to follow up the advantage. The Army of Northern Virginia retreated down the Shenandoah Valley, while McClellan, criticized by the public, and reproached by Lincoln, delayed action and clamored for supplies. The Emancipation Proclamation had been issued (September 22), the mid-term elections had begun, and Lincoln needed a victory. On November 7th the President relieved McClellan of command of the Army of the Potomac, and appointed Ambrose E. Burnside in his place. It was one of the most costly mistakes Lincoln ever made. Burnside was a brave and honest man, an admirable corps commander and conductor of subsidiary operations, but, as he himself feared, simply did not have the grasp of grand strategy which would enable him to direct the movements of a great army.

PAGE 40: *Charge of Humphreys' Division at the Battle of Fredericksburg, Virginia, December 13, 1862.*

Pencil and wash drawing by A. R. Waud.
On light brown paper.
14 1/2 x 21 inches.

PAGE 41: *Gallant Charge of Humphreys' Division at the Battle of Fredericksburg.*

Sketched by A. R. Waud.
Wood engraving.
Harper's Weekly.
Jan. 10, 1863, pp. 24-25.
13 1/2 x 20 inches.

GALLANT CHARGE OF HUMPHREY'S DIVISION AT THE BATTLE OF FREDERICKSBURG.—Sketched by Mr. A. R. Waud.—[See Page 57.]

PAGE 43: *Winter
Campaigning. The Army of
the Potomac on the move.
Sketched near Falmouth–
January 21, 1863.*

1863.
Pencil and wash drawing
by A. R. Waud.
13 7/8 x 20 1/2 inches.

"With the failure of Fredericksburg the nadir of Northern depression seemed to have been reached. Sorrow caused by the death or mutilation of thousands of brave men turned into rage as the people wondered how so fine a fighting instrument as the Army of the Potomac had been used with such stupid futility" (J. G. Randall). Gold went up to 134, and greenbacks depreciated alarmingly. The situation in the army became so dismal that the distracted Burnside asked Lincoln to dismiss some of the best officers, who, like the ranks, lacked faith in their general. After some hesitation, the President approved Burnside's project of another attack across the Rappahannock. The result was the miserable "mud march" of January 20–21st, when the army floundered through a deluge of rain and a slough of adhesive clay, but came no nearer to a vantage-point for attacking Lee. On January 25, Burnside disappeared to his own as well as general relief, and Gen. "Fighting Joe" Hooker took over the wet, cold, and disheartened army.

Alfred Waud's drawing catches with unsurpassable atmosphere the discouragement of the "mud march." The trees, clouds, cloaks, and grasses are whipped by a cruel wind, a baggage wagon lists heavily in the mire, men wade above ankles through the mud, riderless horses struggle in the stream—and still the muffled figures plod forward along the bank and down the farther hill. The banners which waved so bravely against the rebel guns are furled and dejected, and the regiment's dog splashes behind his master, his pessimistic eye on the muddy boot before him, his tail between his legs.

PAGE 45: *Embarkation of Ninth Army Corps at Aquia Creek Landing, February 1863.*

Photograph by
Mathew B. Brady.
6 1/4 x 8 inches.

Until the weather should improve Hooker and the Army of the Potomac marked time along the Rappahannock River. Headquarters were at Falmouth, and the Potomac Flotilla was moored in Aquia Creek, the deep tidal channel which runs into the Potomac about 18 miles north of Fredericksburg. The old river-port was still of some importance and its boat landings still sturdy, although the Union encampment and the cavalry regiment which picketed its horses behind the old seventeenth-century church left it forlorn. Meanwhile, parts of Hooker's command had to be detached to other theaters. Thus on February 4 the Ninth Army Corps, 15,000 strong under Maj. Gen. William F. Smith, received orders to embark for Fort Monroe, "without delay." Maj. Gen. John A. Dix, who commanded the forces holding the Norfolk area, and his second, Gen. John A. Peck at Newport News, were getting nervous about the menacing feints of Gen. Roger A. Pryor and his Confederate troops on the Blackwater. The embarkation which began on February 6 and lasted four days is shown in fairly advanced stage in Brady's photograph.

It is interesting, from the present perfection of photographic technique, to examine the frozen stillness of this picture, and to contrast it with the superb motion in the preceding drawing. Brady had perforce to choose a moment of least action—the sidewheelers cabled, the soldiers sitting, lying, or—if no other position were possible—standing still, the baggage motionless in its heaps, and the rifles stacked about kit bags. The small boy in the foreground—perhaps a young rebel from Aquia, for he does not seem to be in uniform—is fascinated by the tripod and the black cloth beneath which Brady has dived to "catch" this shot.

"Public Resolution No. 9.

Resolved by the Senate and House of Representatives of the United States of America, in Congress assembled, That the gratitude of the American people, and the thanks of their Representatives in Congress, are due, and are hereby tendered . . . to Maj. Gen. George G. Meade, Maj. Gen. Oliver O. Howard, and the officers and soldiers of [the Army of the Potomac], for the skill and heroic valor which, at Gettysburg, repulsed, defeated, and drove back, broken and dispirited, beyond the Rappahannock, the veteran army of the rebellion.

Approved January 28, 1864."

Edwin Forbes' panoramic drawing shows the great battlefield on that third day, July 3, 1863, which decided that the Nation might live. The artist's pencilled notations indicate that the pictures were made at 10 in the morning, while the Union armies held their positions on Round Top, Little Round Top, Cemetery Ridge, and Culp's Hill, facing the gray force on Seminary Ridge.   The fateful grand charge whose failure broke the Confederacy was still over three hours away, but the guns were entrenched and ready. Gen. Henry J. Hunt, chief of the artillery, crossed at about this hour from Culp's Hill to Cemetery Ridge. "Here a magnificent display greeted my eyes. Our whole front for two miles was covered by batteries already in line or going into position. They stretched—apparently in one unbroken mass—from opposite the town to the Peach Orchard, which bounded the view to the left, the ridges of which were planted thick with cannon. Never before had such a sight been witnessed on this continent."

When, about one o'clock, the Confederate batteries opened, the Union Artillery answered Forty-seven regiments waited on Seminary Ridge, 15,000 men, the flower of the South. It seemed madness to send infantry into that fire, but it was the only hope. "General," said George Pickett to Longstreet, "Shall I advance?" Longstreet, unable to speak, nodded. Pickett saluted.

*'I shall go forward, sir,' he said and turned to his
    men.
The commands went down the line. The gray
    ranks started to move.
Slowly at first, then faster, in order, stepping like
    deer;
The Virginians, the fifteen thousand, the
    seventh wave of the tide.*

*There was a death-torn mile of broken ground
    to cross,
And a low stone wall at the end, and behind it
    the Second Corps,
And behind that force another, fresh men who
    had not yet fought.
They started to cross that ground. The guns be-
    gan to tear them.*

*From the hill they say that it seemed more like a
sea than a wave,
A sea continually torn by stones flung out of the
sky,
And yet, as it came, still closing, closing and
rolling on,
As the moving sea closes over the flaws and rips
of the tide.
You could mark the path that they took by the
dead that they left behind,
Spilled from that deadly march as a cart spills
meal on a road,
And yet they came on unceasing, the fifteen
thousand no more,*

*And the blue Virginia flag did not fall, did not
fall, did not fall.*

*Armstead leapt the wall and laid his hand on
the gun,
The last of the three brigadiers who ordered
Pickett's brigades,
He waved his hat on his sword and 'Gave 'em
the steel!' he cried,
A few men followed him over. The rest were
beaten or dead.*

*A few men followed him over. There had been
fifteen thousand
When that sea began its march toward the fish-
hook ridge and the wall.
So they came on in strength, light-footed, stepping like deer,
So they died or were taken. So the iron entered
their flesh.*

(S. V. Benét, *John Brown's Body*.)

PAGES 48 AND 49: *The Battle of Gettysburg: Third Day, July 3rd, 10 am*

Pencil and wash drawing by A. R. Waud. On green tinted paper. 8 x 12 3/4 inches.

PAGE 51: *Appearance of Cemetery hill previous to Pickett's charge.*

Pencil drawing by Edwin Forbes. 9 1/4 x 26 1/4 inches.

artillery & Cemetery Hill previous to Pickett's charge

Entrenched Guns   *Gettysburg on left*

spread over wheel   *Louisiana Tigers charge*   *Stevens' battery*

PAGE 53: *Artist of Harper's Weekly sketching at Gettysburg*.

Photograph by Mathew B. Brady. 8 x 10 inches.

Alfred Waud's drawing was evidently made as the "furious thunderstorm" of the Union cannonade answered the Confederate guns. The photographer Brady—presumably, as in the latest war, the correspondents banded together in emulous friendship—caught him sitting with pad and pencil, slightly protected by a boulder and tree from the line of fire. Alfred R. Waud was not only a fine artist, but a bold man, with a surpassingly splendid beard. A tribute in *Harper's Weekly* at the close of the war eulogizes him and his fellow-artists:

"[They] have not been less busy, and scarcely less imperiled than the soldiers. They have made the weary marches and dangerous voyages. They have shared the soldier's fare: they have ridden and waded, and climbed and floundered, always trusting in lead-pencils and keeping their paper dry. When the battle began, they were there. They drew the enemy's fire as well as our own. The fierce shock, the heaving tumult, the smoky sway of battle from side to side, the line, the assault, the victory—they were a part of all, and their faithful fingers, depicting the scene, have made us a part also."

The Thirty-first Ohio Volunteer Infantry was organized at Camp Chase, Columbus, between August 4 and September 7, 1861. Its colonel was Moses R. Walker. The musician of Company E was named Alfred Edward Mathews. He was 30 years old, strong, adventurous, and could make pictures as well as music. He took his sketchbook to war in his knapsack.

On the 27th of September the new regiment received its orders. As it marched to Cincinnati, an untrained, eager throng, it sang, "We are coming, Father Abraham, five hundred thousand strong." In the city—the largest most of the boys had ever seen—it "received many favors from the citizens." On the 31st it started South. The broad Ohio had been spanned with a pontoon bridge, and the side-wheel river steamers, *Sunny Side* and *Silver Moon* lay by the shore. Colonel Walker on his horse rode before, the long proud line followed over the bridge, and the admiring citizens waved good-bye. The regiment tramped for three days and reached Camp Dick Robinson, near Danville, Ky. Brig. Gen. George H. Thomas reported their arrival in an official report of October 3, and spoke of their embarrassing lack of transportation—"Our supply as yet is very limited, and all the mules have to be broken." On November 4 Brig. Gen. W. T. Sherman, commanding the Department of the Cumberland, wrote of "the raw levies of Ohio and Indiana, who arrive in detachments perfectly fresh from the country and loaded down with baggage, . . . composed of good material, but devoid of company officers of experience," and of the "thorough drill" through which he was putting them.

On December 31, 1862, when Rosecrans' army met Braxton Bragg at Stone River, or Murfreesboro—one of those fierce but indecisive battles typical of the campaign in the West before Grant moved on Vicksburg—the 31st Ohio were still in the main untried. Veterans of long marches through the debatable ground, victims of raids and victors of skirmishes with the rebels, they had not yet been under fire in a pitched field. At Stone River "they acquitted themselves nobly." Artist-musician Mathews probably had time only for mental notes, but he later sketched the charging and firing in exactest detail. Beneath the drawing is quoted a correspondent's account:

"Gen. Rosecrans sent word pressing Gen. McCook to hold the front and he would help him. It would all work right. He now galloped [there he goes, in the exact center of the picture, on a black horse, or maybe farther to the left on a white horse] to the front of Crittenden's left, with his staff, to order the line of battle, when the enemy opened a full battery and emptied two saddles of the escort. Van Cleeves' division was sent to the right, Col. Beatty's Brigade in front. The fire continued to approach on the front with alarming rapidity, extending to the centre, and it was clear that the right was doubling upon the left. The enemy had compelled us to make a complete change of front on that wing and was pressing the centre. Gen. Rosecrans, with splendid daring, dashed into the fire and sent his staff along the lines, starting Beatty's Brigade forward—some six batteries opened and sustained a magnificent fire—directly a tremendous shout was raised along the whole line. The enemy began to fall back rapidly. The general himself urged the troops forward. The rebels thoroughly punished were driven back fully a mile. The same splendid bravery was displayed in the centre, and the whole line advanced."

ALFRED EDWARD MATHEWS remained in the 31st Ohio till the end of his three-year term, September 22, 1864, still a private, and "reduced from musician, transferred to Company A, April 24, 1864." He had found time for sketches, which were elaborated into lithographs. Those of the Siege of Vicksburg, Grant pronounced "the most accurate and true to life I have ever seen. They reflect great credit upon you as a delineator of landscape views." After the war Mathews went on tour in the Middle West with an exhibition of large canvases—Vicksburg, Stone Ridge, Chickamauga, Sherman's March, Lookout Mountain—a "Topogramical Panorama of the War." Then he went

West, and for a time had great success with landscapes and panoramic views of the mighty peaks of the Rockies, the canyons, frontier towns and mining camps. He drew accurately and minutely, correctly placing houses, and buildings, lettering names in, putting pigs and chickens in the streets of Denver, and every spoke in place in the wheels of mining machinery. His first set of western lithographs, *Pencil Sketches of Colorado,* was published in 1866, and he followed it in 1868 with *Pencil Sketches of Montana,* and in 1869 with *Gems of Rocky Mountain Scenery.* The faint blue and tan sketches strike modern eyes as odd and bad, but are of the greatest historical value because of their extraordinary, trivial detail. But the vogue of the brilliant Currier & Ives prints quite overshadowed Mathews, and he soon dropped from public sight. His death was recorded in the briefest of notices in a Boulder, Colo., paper of 1872.

MIDDLETON, STROBRIDGE & Co., originally Middleton, Wallace & Co., were a Cincinnati firm of lithographers who were active from 1855 through the sixties, and produced "a long series of small Civil War views." Mathews also sketched lithographs for the Cincinnati house of Donaldson and Elmes, including some considerably larger views of the fighting around Chattanooga in 1863.

PAGE 56: *The Pontoon Bridge at Cincinnati.*

Sketched by A. E. Mathews.
Tinted Lithograph.
Undated.
15 x 21 inches.

PAGE 57: *The Battle of Stone River or Murfreesboro'. Representing Gen. Sam Beatty's Brigade on December 31, 1862.*

Sketched by A. E. Mathews.
Tinted Lithograph.
Undated.
14 x 20 3/4 inches.

THE PONTOON BRIDGE AT CINCINNATI

The Battle of Stone River or Murfreesboro'.

PAGE 59: *Admiral Porter's Fleet Running the Rebel Blockade of the Mississippi at Vicksburg, April 16, 1863.*

Published by Currier & Ives. Lithograph. 8 x 12 3/8 inches.

The high bluff on which stands the city of Vicksburg, the greatest Confederate stronghold on the Mississippi, dominates the hairpin bend of the great river. There were concentrated the Confederate batteries, making a direct assault from the west inconceivable, while to the north stretched the Yazoo swamps and bayous, impassable to an army. Grant worked out the only approach, a major campaign from the south and east. His Army transferred to the western bank, marched far south, was ferried back across the great water barrier, and now marched through enemy country, without supply bases, over difficult ground, northeastward to Jackson and then doubled back due westward to the siege of Vicksburg. But the lower crossing was dependent on the fleet, and for the fleet there was no choice but to run the gauntlet of the emplanted guns at Vicksburg.

The Currier & Ives, almost as lurid in black and white as in color, figures forth a bombardment quite as furious as Admiral David D. Porter and his ships had to endure. The seven ironclads, each with a coal barge lashed to her side, the captured Confederate ram *General Price* secured to the *Lafayette,* and the three army transports are all named in the print. The ships (not as the designations run, but in order of line) are: Flagship *Benton, Lafayette* and *General Price, Louisville, Mound City, Pittsburg, Carondelet, Silver Wave, Forest Queen, Henry Clay, Tuscumbia.* The caption reads:

"At half past ten P. M. the boats left their moorings & steamed down the river, the *Benton,* Admiral Porter, taking the lead—as they approached the point opposite the town, a terrible concentrated fire of the centre, upper and lower batteries, both water and bluff, was directed upon the channel, which here ran within one hundred yards of the shore. At the same moment innumerable floats of turpentine and other combustible materials were set ablaze. In the face of all this fire, the boats made their way with but little loss except the transport *Henry Clay,* which was set fire & sunk."

FUSCUMBIA.   HENRY CLAY. FOREST QUEEN, SILVER WAVE, CARANDELET, PITTSBURG, MOUND CITY.   LOUISVILLE.   LAFAYETTE & GEN? PRICE.   FLAG SHIP BENTON.

ADMIRAL PORTER'S FLEET RUNNING THE REBEL BLOCKADE OF THE MISSISSIPPI AT VICKSBURG, APRIL 16TH 1863.

At half past ten P.M. the boats left their moorings & steamed down the river, the Benton, Admiral Porter, taking the lead _____ as they approached the point opposite the town, a terrible con_
_entrated fire of the centre, upper and lower batteries, both water and bluff, was directed upon the channel, which here ran within one hundred yards of the shore. At the same moment immense
_le floats of turpentine and other combustible materials were set ablaze. In the face of all this fire, the boats made their way with but little loss except the transport Henry Clay which was set on fire & sunk.

PAGE 61: *The Army of the Potomac–A Sharp -Shooter on Picket Duty.*

From a painting by W. Homer. Wood engraving. Harper's Weekly. Nov. 15, 1862, p. 724. 10 3/4 x 15 1/2 inches.

WINSLOW HOMER (1836–1910) was just trying his way in the art career which was to make him one of the greatest among American painters, when the war came. His boyhood in Cambridge had ended with two years as apprentice to the Boston lithographer, John H. Bufford, and from 1858 he had had his own studio, first in Boston, then after *Harper's Weekly* accepted a drawing, in New York. There he had taken evening classes at the National Academy of Design and worked under a French painter, Rondel. In 1861 Harper's sent him to Washington to make pictures of the inauguration, and afterward to the seat of war in Virginia. He was attached to the staff of the youthful Col. Francis C. Barlow, 61st N. Y. Volunteers, and covered with him the Peninsular campaign, Fair Oaks, Seven Pines, the Wilderness, Malvern Hill. Then he returned to his New York studio and began painting the big war pictures which brought his first real fame. A set of card-size lithographs, "Campaign Sketches," was issued by Prang in 1863, and in the same year he exhibited the "Sharpshooter on Picket Duty," from which this print was made, with several other paintings, at the National Academy. In 1865 he became an Academician. The greatest of his war pictures is generally conceded to be *Prisoners from the Front,* now the property of the Metropolitan Museum of Art, New York, which shows Barlow, "the boy general," inspecting a most heterogeneous batch of four Southerners. *A Sharp-Shooter,* however, will do very well, particularly since it is one instance in which the weeklies' commercial wood engraving did not denature its original, but even provided a quality and an attractiveness all its own.

Wood engraving differs from the woodcut in that the surface of the wood is treated, not with a knife, but with a graver, and to make this possible, the end, across the grain, of a closely-grained piece of wood such as boxwood has to be used. In the hands of its English inventor, the great Thomas Bewick, who made his first attempt in 1779 and had perfected the process before the end of the century, wood engraving was an art. Until about 1832, printing from the blocks had to be done by hand, but by that year technological progress made possible the rapid printing by machine presses, along with type on the same page. As a result commercial wood engravers abandoned the complete transposition of the original which Bewick had achieved, and went in for a humdrum kind of facsimile work. In the case of the *Sharp-Shooter,* however, Homer's painting evidently put the craftsman on his mettle, and the result is handsome and strong.

THE ARMY OF THE POTOMAC—A SHARP-SHOOTER ON PICKET DUTY.—[FROM A PAINTING BY W. HOMER, ESQ.]

Of the cartoonist Thomas Nast, Lincoln remarked, "He has been our best recruiting sergeant." Few issues of the great national magazine, *Harper's Weekly,* from 1862 through the war—and after into the eighties, for that matter—were without a cartoon or other drawing from his spirited and able pen. His political caricature was without question one of the greatest influences in American journalism of the period.

THOMAS NAST (1840–1902) was the son of a German regimental musician, born in the barracks of the 9th Bavarian Regiment at Landau, Germany. He was brought to New York in 1846, and as a schoolboy began his drawings and went to art classes. Frank Leslie, publisher of *Leslie's Illustrated Newspaper,* discovered him when he was 15, and engaged him at $4 a week. In 1859 his first important political cartoon appeared in *Harper's Weekly*. He left Leslie's for the *New York Illustrated News,* and for

them covered John Brown's funeral and other important assignments. In 1860 he went to England to sketch a big prize fight, but was attracted by the more serious business of Garibaldi's campaign to Italy. He came back to America just before the war, and quickly found himself a correspondent in the field. In the summer of 1862, Fletcher Harper engaged him as a staff artist, urging him to make pictures with ideas rather than battle reports.

Nast's greatest work, of course, is to be found in his cartoons and propaganda pieces, but these do not fall into the scheme of our Album. His reportorial battle pieces are inchoate and inferior. We have, therefore, compromised by reproducing from *Harper's* two characteristic picture groups on representative Civil War themes, which are in part fact and in part idea, sentimentally treated. One, *The Press in the Field,* has a special relationship to the subject-matter of this book.

THE PRESS ON THE FIELD.

CONTRABAND NEWS.

IN ACTION.

RELIABLE INFORMATION.

OFF TO THE WAR.

HOME AGAIN.

REGIMENT.

IN ACTION.

NEWS FROM HOME.

WRITING HOME.

THE DRUMMER

HIS TOILET.

THE REGIMENT'S FAVORITE.

IN CAMP.

HIS DAILY BREAD.

BOY OF OUR

THE DRUMMER BOY OF OUR REGIMENT.—LIGHT WAR SCENES.

On the Southern side, the Baltimore artist John Adalbert Volck endeavored to counteract Nast's influence by his own series of caricatures, published under the pseudonym of V. Blada, [*Adalbe*rt backward]. Lincoln and Benjamin F. Butler were the chief targets of his attack—Butler had imprisoned him in 1861—and later reproductions of his savage cartoons served materially in the political general's defeat for the governorship of Massachusetts in 1871. Notable among the "Blada" series is the drawing of Lincoln and Butler as "Don Quixote and Sancho Panza." The book of *Confederate War Etchings* from which the two prints are taken contains 29 plates, divided between political caricature and typical military scenes, and is his most important collection.

Volck, like Nast, was a Bavarian, born at Augsburg in 1828. A student of dentistry at the Polytechnic Institute of Nürnberg, he became involved in the Revolution of 1848 and fled to America. He went first to St. Louis, then tried his fortune in the gold rush. More solid results were attained in his profession; in 1851 he became an instructor in the Baltimore College of Dental Surgery. He was a prominent dentist, a pioneer in the use of porcelain fillings, and a founder of the Association of Dental Surgeons.

Unlike most of the German refugees of 1848, and in an unexplained manner, Volck became an ardent Southern sympathizer, and besides the caricature series did illustrations for a number of Confederate books, during and after the war. In 1870 he painted a portrait in oils of General Lee, which is now in the Valentine Museum in Richmond. The head of Jefferson Davis on the 10-cent stamp of the Confederacy is often attributed to him, but was more probably done by his brother, Frederick, a sculptor. Later, he worked in bronze and silver—a shield in memory of the Confederate women is in the Confederate Museum in Richmond. One of the founders of the famous Wednesday Club, he was a well-known and popular figure in Baltimore until his death in 1912.

It is difficult to say why Volck resorted to the technique of *etching* for reproducing these simple line drawings; his plates are certainly very unremarkable specimens of that noble art. The best of them, from a purely aesthetic standpoint, is indubitably *Vicksburg Canal,* but since the original drawing for this has been reproduced in the *American Battle Painting* catalogue, and differs only very slightly from the etching, we have chosen instead two pieces in which, at this early date, Volck seizes upon two themes long characteristic of Southern sentiment.

A noticeable feature of Volck's etchings of Southern scenes is that he had the least possible comprehension of Negro physiognomy. This is conspicuous in the frightened child on the floor of the slave cabin in *Slaves Concealing Their Master.* The mammy, mainly because of the traditional headdress, is somewhat more convincing.

Prayer in Stonewall Jackson's Camp is no masterpiece, but it does summarize a whole phase of the Civil War. Through the efforts of the Bible Societies, the Tract Societies, and church publishing houses, the Confederate armies in 1861 and 1862 were flooded with religious literature. In 1863 began the great religious revivals in camps. Bell Irvin Wiley tells us in his *Life of Johnny Reb* that the revivals in Jackson's corps started early in March, and quotes a private's letter of April 12:

"Gen Jackson (God Bless him) has given us the privilege to be exempt from Morning's Drill in order that we may attend preaching . . . we have two sermons each day & although we have no church to worship in we all sit around on the ground and listen to the sweet sound of the Gospel."

Gen. Thomas J. Jackson, Lee's right-hand man—"I know not how to replace him," wrote Lee after the fatal accident in the twilight on the victorious field of Chancellorsville—was himself a devoted Presbyterian. After Bull Run he was hero and legend to the South and to his adoring soldiers, who cheered wildly whenever "Old Jack" came in sight. The piety of this figure out of the Old Testament was well known in the Army of Virginia. "On the eve of battle, he would rise several times during the night for prayer, and he was so strict in his observance of the Sabbath that he would not even write a letter to his wife when he thought it would travel in the mails on Sunday. His favorite company was that of Presbyterian divines; his chosen topic of conversation was theology" (*Dictionary of American Biography*). He stands at the left in Volck's drawing, his hands folded in prayer, the eyes that flashed with intense excitement in action now stern and raised to a stern God of Battles.

PAGE 68: *Slaves Concealing their Master from a Search Party.*

From Adalbert John Volck. Confederate War Etchings, No. 12. Etching. 4 7/8 x 7 1/8 inches.

PAGE 69: *Prayer in Stonewall Jackson's Camp.*

From Adalbert John Volck. Confederate War Etchings, No. 24. Etching. 4 7/8 x 7 1/8 inches.

PAGE 71: *Going into Camp at Night.*

1876.
by Edwin Forbes.
Etching, printed in sepia.
11 x 15 7/8 inches.

PAGE 73: *Infantry Soldier on Guard. [Sergeant William J. Jackson.]*

1876.
by Edwin Forbes.
Etching, printed in sepia.
11 x 15 7/8 inches.

EDWIN FORBES, staff illustrator for *Frank Leslie's Illustrated Newspaper* from 1861 to 1865, is known entirely through his war drawings. The best of them were collected in the volume of copper-plate etchings, *Life Studies of the Great Army,* in which *Going into Camp* is the twenty-first plate. The set received an award at the Centennial Exposition in Philadelphia in the year of its publication. Forbes, a New Yorker, was born in 1839 and lived till 1895, when he died in Flatbush. After the war he continued to trade on his sketches of camp and battle life, illustrating in the same hasty manner a number of children's stories. In 1891 he wrote his reminiscences, *Thirty Years After, An Artist's Story of the Great War,* an entertainingly chatty text to accompany his remaining sketches. For several years before his death he was paralyzed on one side, and painted and wrote with his left hand. This may possibly account for the curious circumstance of his wife's signature on Plate 21.

The list of titles for the plates in *Life Studies of the Great Army* bears explanatory legends. *Going into Camp at Night* is glossed: "The fields on all sides are covered with troops who are engaged in cooking supper, the column in the road marching on and disappearing over the hill in the distance."

Forbes had begun his art study in 1857 by specializing in animal painting, and then had turned to *genre* and landscape. Few of his sketches are portraits, and of those few, most are stiff and wooden; but the sketch of Sgt. William J. Jackson, a solemn lad with his arm resting on his rifle, has a direct emotional appeal considerably beyond that of Forbes' crowded scenes. Sergeant Jackson is young but toughened by campaigning; the sorry fortunes of the ill-generalled Army of the Potomac have led him to expect little, but it is not likely that rebel raiders will knock out Stoneman's Switch without paying a stiff price for it.

PAGE 75: *Fort Albany, at Arlington Heights*.

1862.
Published by E. F. Ruhl
Lithograph,
printed in color.
12 3/4 x 19 1/2 inches.

Fort Albany, just below the turn from Arlington Ridge Road into the old Columbia Turnpike on Arlington Heights, was the fourth of the fortifications erected on the Virginia side for the defense of Washington. On May 23, 1861, three columns of the volunteer army crossed the Potomac—one by the Georgetown Aqueduct, one by water to Alexandria, the third across the Long Bridge, at the foot of Fourteenth Street. This last was under Maj. Gen. Samuel P. Heintzelman, commanding the New York Volunteers. He reported:

"We advanced with the 25th N. Y. on the Columbia turnpike and took post between Roach's and Dr. Antisell . . . The 25th N. Y. S. M. was posted at the toll-gate and Vose's Hill on the Columbia turnpike."

By dawn of next day ground was broken for Fort Corcoran below the Aqueduct and Fort Runyon just across the Long Bridge—on about the site where in a later struggle the largest war office in the world has placed its Pentagon Building—but it was a week more before Fort Albany was laid out and its construction commenced. The buildings and works were put up by the 25th N. Y. Regiment on the spot where they had encamped, and there a part of the Army of the Potomac wheeled and turned practising the formations which prepared them to break the charge at Malvern Hill and face the fire of Fredericksburg. The fort is described in the report of a commission of Engineers to the Secretary of War late in 1862:

"*Fort Albany* is a work partly bastioned, well built and in admirable condition; the parapets being turfed and the scarps revetted with boards. It is well defiladed and in a very advantageous position to cover the Long Bridge and look into the gorges of Forts Richardson and Craig. It sees the high ground in front of Fort Tillinghast and commands the valley between Forts Richardson and Scott. It is well provided with magazines, embrasures, and bomb-proofs. Some heavy rifled pieces are required."

It will be noted that there is no lithographic artist or printer named on this view, but only the Albany publisher, E. F. Ruhl. It may be guessed that Ruhl had commissioned one of the larger houses to produce a print which could be most widely marketed in Albany; or that one of these houses had selected him as their Albany agent in the local marketing of a series of such views.

1. Rifle Comp.? Cap.? F. Newdorf.	5. Toll Gate.		FORT ALBANY,		9. Well.	13. Lafayette Guard, Lieut. G. Godefroy.
2. Light Infantry, Cap.? J.J. Huber.	6. Blacksmith Shop.		AT ARLINGTON HEIGHTS		10. Artillery, Cap.? J. Fredendall.	14. City Volunteers, Cap.? Frank Marshall.
3. Emmet Guard, Cap.? H. Mulholland.	7. Roche's Farm.		ERECTED 1861 BY THE 25TH REGIMENT, N.Y.S.M.		11. Field & Staff Officers.	15. Worth Guard, Cap.? J. Gray.
4. Montgomery Guard, Lieut. T. McDermott.	8. Doctor's House.		Colonel M.K. BRYAN.		12. Musicians.	16. Burgesses Corps, Cap.? H. Kingsley.
			Lieut. Colonel J. SWIFT.	Major D. FRIEDLANDER.		

76

PAGE 77: *Commissary Department. Encampment of the Mass. 6th Regiment of Volunteers at the Relay House near Baltimore, Maryland.*

From a sketch by Alfred Ordway. Published by J. H. Bufford. Tinted lithograph. 9 x 13 5/8 inches.

The proud Sixth Massachusetts Regiment of Volunteer Militia, "first to offer its services; first to reach its State's capital; first to reach the nation's capital; first to inflict suffering on traitors; first to attest its sincerity with its blood" (*Historical Sketch of the Old Sixth Regiment,* by John W. Hanson, Chaplain, 1866), was also the first regiment of the war to see its commissary tent set up on the march, complete with market building and supply tent, signs from home on the trees, and sides of beef beneath the butcher's knife. The encampment at the Relay House, near Baltimore, here sketched by Alfred Ordway, lasted only two hours on April 19—4 days after Lincoln's call for volunteers—but the boys, risen in the Concord and Lexington tradition from Middlesex, Essex, Suffolk, and Worcester Counties, were already veterans. Within two days they had mustered at Lowell, Boston, and Worcester, and entrained for the South. At New York, Jersey City, and Philadelphia, huge ovations awaited them, thousands of people lining the tracks, and making "all possible demonstrations of applause."

In the early morning of April 19 they crossed the Mason and Dixon line—the first Yanks to invade the Southland. And at Baltimore there waited another crowd, this time a mob with stones and pistols. Four Massachusetts soldiers lay dead and 36 bore wounds for the Union when that shed, the "Washington Market," was taken over by the commissary, the sign of "Bay State House" tacked up, and dinner cooked. By suppertime they were in Washington.

An interesting touch in Ordway's sketch is the white headdress, the "havelock," worn by the soldier on the right, a phenomenon of 1861. The "name came from the designer, the British General, Sir Henry Havelock, whose troops suffered from exposure in India." Made of heavy white drilling, they hung in long flaps over the soldiers' necks.

The lithographer JOHN H. BUFFORD worked in this profession from at least 1835 until after 1871. He had begun as an apprentice under William S. Pendleton in Boston, but about 1835 went to New York, where he worked for Endicott and Nathaniel Currier. In 1841 he went back to set up his own lithographing firm in Boston, where he became one of the principal American lithographers, publishing a great number of prints and issuing catalogs. He is most often recalled in connection with his apprentice, Winslow Homer, who got his professional start in Bufford's shop.

ALFRED ORDWAY (1819–97), the Boston landscape artist who sketched the scene at the Relay House, may also have exerted an influence on the young Homer whose reputation was so far to outshine his own.

PAGE 79: *Funeral of Colonel Vosburgh–The Hearse approaching the Railroad Depot.*

Undated.
Pencil and wash drawing
by A. R. Waud.
10 1/2 x 14 3/4 inches.

On May 22, 1861, in Richmond a Confederate correspondent noted, "Flags halfmast yesterday [presumably in Washington] for the death of Col. Vosburgh, 71st N. Y. Regt." The funeral procession which Alfred Waud sketched as it passed from the navy yard toward the railway depot on the Mall below the capitol, must have been the first of many such cortèges to take its sad and stately way through the Washington streets during the war, and was probably much more elaborate than those in its later stages. Interesting points in this impressive drawing are the dome of the Capitol, still under construction, the riderless horse led behind the hearse, and the Zouave uniforms of the military escort.

Abram S. Vosburgh had been since 1852 colonel of the "American Rifles," of the old New York State Militia, the predecessor of the 71st Regiment. This regiment, known as "Second Excelsior Brigade," had signed at once in 1861 as three-month volunteers. With 950 men, Vosburgh sailed on April 21 in the vanguard from New York for the defense of Washington. But the gallant charge at Fair Oaks, the chief glory of the 71st N. Y., was ordered by another leader; Vosburgh died of a hemorrhage of the lungs in his bed at the Navy Yard on May 20. In fact he had no business to take the field at all.

Both as first officer casualty of the New York volunteers, and as a leading citizen, Colonel Vosburgh received distinguished honors. *Harper's Weekly* of June 8, 1861, carries an illustration of a magnificent funeral parade in New York City, where he was buried on May 23. It was led by two regiments of cavalry and detachments of at least five regiments, and followed by an escort of the 71st, the Home Guard, and "Tammany Society of which the deceased was a member."

A few days later in Washington came the funeral procession of the young and vastly popular Col. Elmer E. Ellsworth of the New York Fire Zouaves, shot down by a secessionist innkeeper as he removed the Confederate flag from the Marshall House in Alexandria, which town his regiment had been sent to occupy. Washington, not yet inured to daily violent death, was plunged in mourning.

Funeral of Col ____

PAGE 81: *Skedaddler's Hall, Harrison's Landing.*

July 3, 1862
Pencil and wash drawing
by A. R. Waud.
On brown tinted paper.
10 x 14 1/4 inches.

Harrison's Landing on the James River was the base to which McClellan transferred his army before winning the victory of Malvern Hill during the Peninsular Campaign. In that battle of July 1, 1862, the "brilliant conduct" of the "Excelsior Brigade" (72d N. Y.) was especially noticed by General Hooker. So it is a false impression that is given by the soldiers' appellation, "Skedaddler's Hall" where on July 3d the valiant warriors are sketched taking their ease.

"To skedaddle," meaning "to retire hastily, to decamp," or in plainer words, to run away, was a bit of Civil War soldiers' argot that replaced an earlier favorite verb, "to absquatulate." The *New York Tribune* on the 10th of August 1861, regarded it as confined to enemy behavior: "No sooner did the traitors discover their approach than they 'skidaddled' (a phrase the Union boys up here apply to the good use the seceshers make of their legs in time of danger)." Apparently "Skedaddler's Hall" was the nickname for the 1862 version of a U. S. O. center, where the first to retire from action may have found the softest seats. Like much other Civil War slang, the word has found a lasting, though now somewhat archaic, place in the American language.

PAGE 83: *A Sutler's Tent.*

August 1862
Pencil and wash drawing
by A. R. Waud.
On gray tinted paper.
10 x 14 1/4 inches.

In his exhaustive study, *The Organization and Administration of the Union Army, 1861–65,* Fred Albert Shannon speaks of the various camp followers, "grafters, pay-discount sharks, gamblers and sutlers . . . ever ready to relieve the soldier of any inconvenient burden of money." Others came and went, but "sutlers were an ever-present evil." Their tents or booths were set up in each encampment, and there only could the soldier go for any relief from the monotonous army fare. The rations were one pound of "hardtack," one and one-quarter pounds of fresh or salt beef or three-quarters of a pound of bacon, beans, rice or hominy, and coffee. Such delicacies as fruit, cheese, butter, jam, and above all tobacco, could be had only by recourse to the sutlers. Beer and whiskey they sold publicly or in private. They were protected in their trade by the government, no other salesmen peddling their commodities being permitted in the camps. Concessions to sutlers were usually secured in their states through political influence, and they enjoyed a semiofficial connection with the regiments. Their charges were what the traffic would bear—60 cents for a pound of cheese, a dollar a plug for tobacco, $1.00 or $1.25 for a can of fruit, 15 cents for cigars.

By the autumn of 1861 congressional legislation was needed to straighten out the difficulties of soldiers and sutlers. The camp merchants fought against its enactment. An act of December 24, 1861, repealed the earlier legislation that had allowed the sutlers to attach monthly pay; but in March 1862 this was changed to permit a slight lien. The final provision was that "no sutler could sell to any soldier on credit to the extent of more than a quarter of his month's pay each month and his legal claim was to be only one-sixth." Sale of intoxicants was forbidden. A board of officers in each regiment was appointed to fix prices, which they did with infinite diversity and frequent cases of split profits. The soldiers naturally rejoiced when the Enrollment Act of 1863 specifically stated that sutlers were not to be exempt from the draft.

Alfred Waud's drawing was made five months after passage of the act of March 1862, but apparently this sutler was doing as he pleased about the limitation on whiskey. Were the double-X bottles opened for privates as well as for officers? Beside the partly-cut cheese on the shelf hang the scales, for which the artist may have felt as much distrust as does the soldier turning resignedly away with his bundle.

PAGE 85: *Confederate Camp, during the late American War.*

1871.
After the painting by C.W. Chapman.
by M &N Hanhart.
Published by Louis Zimmer.
Chromolithograph.
10 1/8 x 15 1/4 inches.

CONRAD WISE CHAPMAN, of whose work the *Confederate Camp* is one of the finest and most polished examples, was by profession an artist and the son of an artist. His father, John Gadsby Chapman of Virginia, was an Academician, a distinguished portrait, historical and landscape painter, illustrator, etcher and wood engraver. The father's textbook on drawing, *Chapman's Drawing Book,* was familiar to all art students of the time, and his panel of the "Baptism of Pocahontas" is in the rotunda of the Capitol at Washington. He went to live in Rome in 1848, when his son Conrad was six years old. The 19-year-old, romantic boy was beginning to paint under his father's tutelage in Italy when the war broke out. He at once rushed home to America, worked his way West from New York, and joined a Kentucky regiment. A violent partisan, he was conspicuous for courage. At Shiloh he received a bad head wound, from which he never fully recovered. Through his father's influence he was transferred to General Wise's brigade, where he held the nominal rank of ordnance sergeant.

Wise's brigade was sent to Charleston, S. C., and there Chapman was detailed to make paintings of the fortifications of Charleston Harbor. The 31 paintings that resulted are among the treasures of the Confederate Museum in Richmond. It was perhaps at this time that he also painted the picture of camp life from which this elegant colored lithograph, produced in England, was made. The live oaks and pine trees dripping with grey moss suggest a locale in the deep South. Chapman made other pictures of camp life, microscopically fine and delicate in detail, as well as portrait sketches of Confederate soldiers and officers.

In December 1864, he was given leave to go to Rome with Bishop Lynch of Charleston, and ran the blockade. In the spring of 1865 he started to return, but on the way back learned of the fall of the Confederacy. He drifted down to Mexico and there did more painting as well as taking part in the troubles of Maximilian's day. The old wound in his head bothered him, and the fear of being considered a deserter preyed on his romantic temperament. When he went back to Rome and to art he lost his mind. He eventually recovered, lived in Mexico, and came back to Richmond hoping to enlist in the Spanish-American War, but was rejected as too old. He tried Mexico again, then New York, and finally came home, very poor and proud, to die in Virginia. A few years before his death (1910) he gave his remaining pictures and those of his father to the State of Virginia. They are now in the Virginia State Library.

PAGE 87: *Mustered Out.*

Pencil and wash drawing
by A. R. Waud.
On green tinted paper.
9 3/4 x 14 1/4 inches.

No note can be found as to where Waud sketched this proud and happy homecoming scene. From the numbers of wives, sweethearts, and offspring, it may be assumed to be one of the Southern or border States. Free Negroes had from the first tried to enlist, both in Confederate and Union armies. After the Emancipation Proclamation (September 22, 1862), Lincoln authorized four Negro regiments, and the total enrollment of Negroes in the Federal forces during the war approximated 200,000. The larger part were recruited in Confederate territory. They were used mainly for garrison duty, guarding lines of communication and the like, but at the Petersburg Crater, Fort Pillow and other battlefields, they fought bravely. *A History of the Negro Troops in the War of the Rebellion,* by Col. George W. Williams (1888), expresses the metamorphosis of the Negro in glowing language:

"The part enacted by the Negro soldier in the war of the Rebellion is the romance of North American history. It was midnight and noonday without a space between; from the Egyptian darkness of bondage to the lurid glare of civil war; from clanking chains to clashing arms; from passive submission to the cruel curse of slavery to the brilliant aggressiveness of a free soldier; from a chattel to a person; from the shame of degradation to the glory of military exaltation; and from deep obscurity to fame and martial immortality."

It is pleasing to have evidence in Waud's sketch that the reward of the Negro soldiers was not limited to glory and military exaltation. The mustering-out process here includes a file into the building auspiciously marked "Banking Office." Alfred Waud, an Englishman by birth, appears from this and other sketches to have found in the negro countenance a source of innocent merriment.

At Philadelphia the troops from the Northern States changed trains. The railroad brought them to Camden and ferries took them across the river to the foot of Washington Avenue, where the Philadelphia, Wilmington and Baltimore Railroad had its station near the Navy Yard. The soldiers arrived hungry. On May 26 and May 27, 1861, two "refreshment saloons—free" were opened by the patriotic Philadelphians. Both were volunteer organizations, supported by private contributions, and both kept up their work throughout the war. The larger of the two, the Union Volunteer Refreshment Saloon, was the better known, feeding nearly 900,000 soldiers through the four years of war, but the Cooper Shop Volunteer Refreshment Saloon beat its competitor by one day in its official opening. Mr. William M. Cooper and Mr. Henry W. Pearce, partners in an "oak-cooper's" (barrel manufacturer's) firm, were the leading spirits, provided one of their buildings on Otsego Street, just southwest of Washington Avenue, and stand in the forefront of the Philadelphia lithograph, not averse to the free advertising afforded by public philanthropy and patriotism.

The gentlemen of the committee stood for their portraits in front, but the ladies, who blushed at showing their faces in a public scene—note in the "Exterior View" above how many of his ladies the artist has drawn in hoop-skirted and shawled rear views—contributed unceasingly of their time and skill. As a troop train left Jersey City, day or night, a telegram was sent to the Union, and a small cannon fired. Like the O. C. D. volunteers of 1942–43 at the "blue" siren signal, the ladies poured out and hurried to the rival sheds, where they began cooking. Small boys watched the river bank and rushed up to call for the second gun when the boats came in sight.

A soldier's letter home, dated June 1, 1863, describes what followed:

"Dear Parents:—I will endeavor to give you a faint description of our reception in Philadelphia, but I know that my pen cannot half do justice to the subject, but I do know that the remembrance of it will live in the hearts of our brave artillery boys as long as they are able to train a gun or draw a sword in the defence of their country. As soon as we reached the city we marched to the dining saloon, about ten or fifteen rods from the ferry. As soon as we got there we entered the washroom, a room large enough to accommodate sixty or seventy men to wash at a time. Then we marched into a splendid hall, with room enough to feed five hundred men at a time. There were gentlemen to wait on us, and they would come around and ask if we had plenty and urge us to eat more. We had nice white bread, beautiful butter, cold boiled ham, cheese, coffee, with plenty of milk and sugar . . . After we had eaten our fill, which was considerable, for we had eaten nothing since morning, we returned to the streets. Our knapsacks on the sidewalk were left without a guard, but they were almost covered with little children who were watching to see that no one disturbed them . . . It seemed that the people could not do us enough honor . . ."

The two Volunteer Refreshment Saloons did not limit their USO service to food, but each maintained a small hospital as well. Letter paper, stamps, "Soldiers' Guides," Bibles, prayer books and tracts, and even daily newspapers were given to any boy who asked, and there were occasional entertainments, and religious services on Sundays.

To see that their good works were not hidden under a bushel, Messrs. Cooper and Fort commissioned a large chromolithograph from Morris H. Traubel & Co. Like many of the Philadelphia and Cincinnati lithographers, Traubel (1820–97) was of German birth, and had learned lithography in his native city of Frankfurt am Main. In business in Philadelphia from his thirtieth year, and by himself from 1854 to 1869, Traubel successfully applied the new methods of color or chromolithography.

PAGE 91: *Interior View of the Cooper Shop Volunteer Refreshment Saloon, the first opened for Union Volunteers in the United States.*

1862.
Printed by M.H. Traubel.
Chromolithograph.
32 1/4 x 19 3/4 inches.

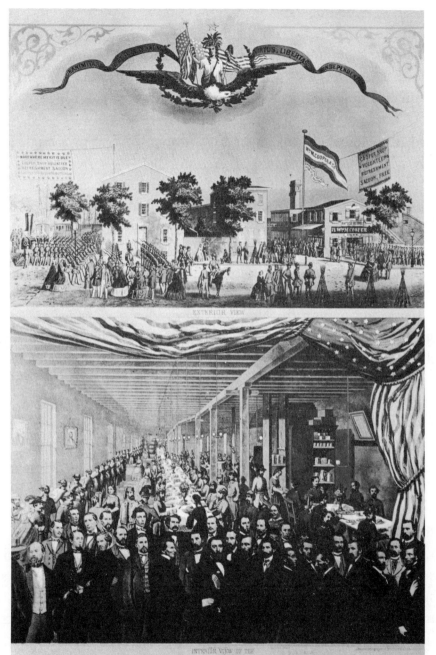

EXTERIOR VIEW

INTERIOR VIEW OF THE
COOPER SHOP VOLUNTEER REFRESHMENT SALOON,
THE FIRST OPENED FOR UNION VOLUNTEERS IN THE UNITED STATES.
1009 Otsego St.   PHILADELPHIA.

The first wounded of the war, streaming back from Bull Run, met an appalling lack of preparation. The antiquated Army Medical Bureau had no hospitals, few nurses, and pitifully small supplies of food, clothing and medicines. Churches, halls, and warehouses were turned into hurried substitutes for hospital wards, while charitable ladies gathered in relief societies. To meet an acute need the United States Sanitary Commission was formed in June 1861. This most important of all organizations for war relief, which absorbed most of the local Aid Societies, was supported by private contributions, church offerings, and "Sanitary Fairs" throughout the North. Its work, directed by its able secretary, Frederick Law Olmsted, and carried on before the end of the war by 500 agents, covered all forms of aid—in field, camp, and hospital, transportation, nursing, inspection, relief to the disabled, and care of dependent families.

Large on the list of the Sanitary Commission's charges bulked the convalescent soldiers. The trains and troop ships after every battle unloaded in Washington and the other cities crowds of disabled men, too exhausted and weak to go on with their regiments, yet not so desperately wounded as to be allowed hospitalization. Streets were filled with stragglers and walking wounded. Convalescents were discharged from the overcrowded hospitals still weak and ill, far from home and penniless.

The Sanitary Commission established soldiers' lodges to care for these victims of war.

In Washington and in nearby Alexandria, where the first tide of retreat from the battle front in Virginia rolled in its flood, the lodges were placed near the depots. There hot meals were served, first aid given, and the soldiers sorted out, housed, and cared for till ready to return to their regiments, or provided with money to make their painful way home. In the picture of the Alexandria Soldiers' Rest, the receiving lodge is right beside the station, a long shed, with the name of the Sanitary Commission above it. Soldiers pile into it from the train. Farther on, in a big enclosure dominated by a huge flagpole, stand the rows of barracks which the poor convalescents called "Camp Misery."

By 1863 the Army Medical Service had undergone reorganization and with the aid of the Sanitary Commission was establishing general military hospitals. Miss Dorothea Dix, appointed Superintendent of Female Nurses by the Surgeon General in June 1861, had organized her staffs of devoted women. Typical of the buildings erected was the Patterson Park General Hospital in Baltimore, which is pictured in the second print—long barracklike rows around a court, with fairly adequate windows and balconies. For the interior scene in such hospitals, Walt Whitman has left his testimony:

"There is a long building appropriated to each ward. Let us go into ward 6. It contains to-day, I should judge, eighty or a hundred patients, half sick, half wounded. The edifice is nothing but boards, well whitewash'd inside, and the usual slender-framed iron bedsteads, narrow and plain. You walk down the central passages, with a row on either side, their feet towards you, and their heads to the wall. There are fires in large stoves, and the prevailing white of the walls is reliev'd by some ornaments, stars, circles, etc., made of evergreens. The view of the whole edifice and occupants can be taken at once, for there is no partition. You may hear groans or other sounds of unendurable suffering from two or three of the cots, but in the main there is quiet—almost a painful absence of demonstration; but the pallid face, the dul'd eye, and the moisture on the lip, are demonstration enough" (*Specimen Days in America*).

And in *Drum Taps*, "The Wound Dresser":

Bearing the bandages, water and sponge,
Straight and swift to my wounded I go . . .
To the long rows of cots up and down each
*   side I return,*
To each and all one after another I draw
*   near, not one do I miss,*
An attendant follows holding a tray, he car-
*   ries a refuse pail,*
Soon to be fill'd with clotted rags and blood,
*   emptied, and fill'd again.*

I onward go, I stop,
With hinged knees and steady hand to dress
*   wounds,*
I am firm with each, the pangs are sharp yet
*   unavoidable,*
One turns to me his appealing eyes—poor
*   boy! I never knew you,*
Yet I think I could not refuse this moment to
*   die for you, if that would save you.*

On, on I go, (open doors of time! open hos-
*   pital doors!)*
The crush'd head I dress, (poor crazed hand
*   tear not the bandage away,)*
The neck of the cavalry-man with the bullet
*   through and through I examine,*
Hard the breathing rattles, quite glazed al-
*   ready the eye, yet life struggles hard,*
(Come sweet death! be persuaded O beauti-
*   ful death!*
In mercy come quickly.)

Soldiers Rest was turned out by CHARLES MAGNUS & Co., a New York lithographic house with a Washington branch at 520 Seventh Street. They specialized in letterheads and views, but during the Civil War brought out a great body of war scenes. The firm lasted from 1858 through the 1870's, and aimed at timeliness rather than any more enduring quality in their output.

PAGE 94: *Soldiers Rest, Alexandria, Virginia.*

1864.
Published
by Charles Magnus & Co.
Lithograph, colored by hand.
10 3/4 x 16 3/4 inches.

PAGE 95: *U.S.A. General Hospital Patterson Park, Baltimore, Maryland*

1863.
Printed by E. Sachse & Co.
Lithograph, printed in color.
11 x 17 inches.

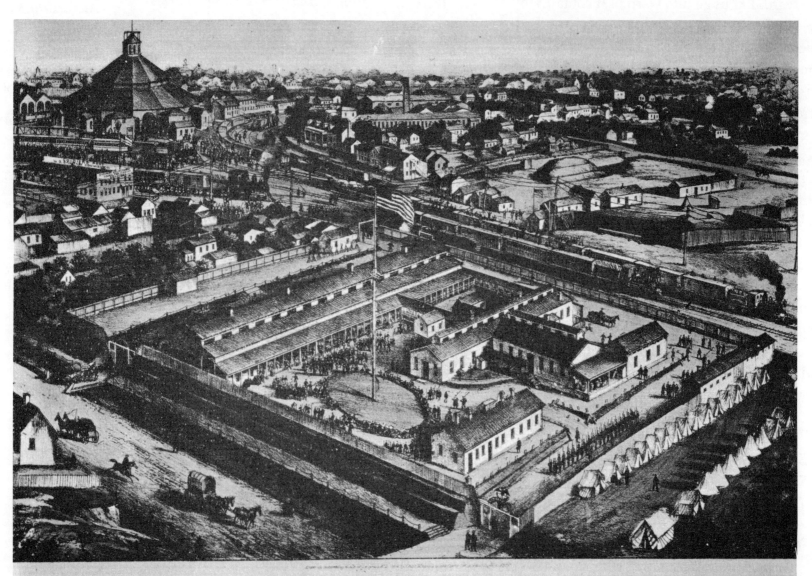

SOLDIERS REST, ALEXANDRIA, VA

COMMANDED BY CAPT. JOHN J. HOFF

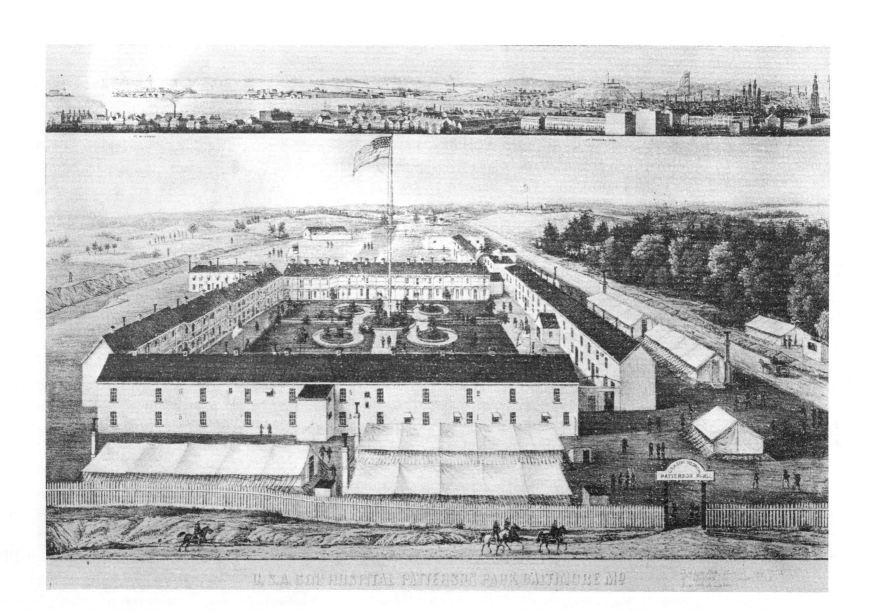

U.S.A. GEN'L HOSPITAL PATTERSON PARK BALTIMORE MD

The tragic condition of prisoners, Union and Confederate, is remembered as perhaps the most cruel aspect of the long civil strife. Out of the vituperation and recriminations on both sides, and from close study of official reports, the historians have sifted a few facts. "Professor Channing concludes that 'each government cared for its enemy prisoners about as well as . . . for its own soldiers'; while Dr. Hesseltine pointed out that each side displayed mismanagement, congestion and unfitness of officer personnel, and that in the North as well as the South one finds disease, filth, depression, disorder, vermin, poor food, lack of elementary sanitation, and as a result, intolerable misery and death on an appalling scale" (J. G. Randall). The difficulties of exchange and release were such that no enduring plan could be worked out. A cartel arranged on July 22, 1862, for the exchange of prisoners soon broke down because of many such complications as those of parole and the Confederate refusal to exchange Negro soldiers. From 1863 on enormous numbers of prisoners were taken and held by both sides. Official reports show that, without reckoning captured men released on the field, the Confederates took nearly 195,000 Union prisoners and the Federals about 215,000 Confederates. "The embarrassment of the South, especially in the later part of the war, in attempting to care for these hordes of captives at a time when its own transportation and supply system was broken down . . . must be remembered in judging the admittedly frightful conditions which existed at Andersonville, Belle Isle, and Salisbury."

In January 1862, the Confederate prison at Salisbury, N. C., was opened. Prisoners taken at Bull Run and succeeding battles of 1861, who had been crowded at Richmond, were sent to the site, an abandoned cotton factory, with neighboring buildings, formerly boarding houses, shaded by a grove of oaks, the whole surrounded by a board fence. Food in 1862 was fairly plentiful, though the prisoners pronounced the beef to be horse or mule. By the time of Jackson's victories in the Shenandoah Valley early that year, the prison was too crowded to receive more occupants. The Union soldiers were released under the cartel of exchange in the late summer, and the prison was continued for political prisoners and deserters. There were 800 of these when in early October 1864, 7,500 Yankee captives from the horribly overcrowded Richmond prison, Belle Isle, were transferred there.

"Salisbury on a smaller scale reproduced all the defects of Andersonville," comments Dr. Hesseltine. There was a scarcity of water, unbearable stench, only 11 acres of red clay mud; the rations, like those of the Confederacy itself in that bleak year, were all too meagre; the local wheat crop failed. Disease was prevalent; "from October 1864 to February 1865, 3,479 prisoners died out of a total of 10,321 confined there."

OTTO BOETTICHER's picture has nothing to do with the horrors of the Salisbury prison camp. There is a fence, it is true, but the men strolling, sitting, lying, smoking and sporting in the enclosure all seem sufficiently clad, sturdy and cheerful. The new national game is going spiritedly forward in the center of an apparently contented ring. Captain Boetticher was at the camp only for a few months in 1862, at a time when conditions were not yet out of hand. The Muster Rolls show that he was captured on March 29 and exchanged for a Confederate of equal rank, Capt. F. Culbertson, 7th Virginia, at Aiken's Landing on September 30.

The 68th New York Volunteer Regiment of Infantry, a largely German organization of which Boetticher was a member, was raised at the call for three-year volunteers in July 1861. On July 22d, Col. R. J. Belge, of New York City, received authority from the War Department to recruit a regiment. The New York Muster Rolls show that Otto Boetticher, age 45 years, was enrolled on July 22, and mustered in as Captain, Co. G, on August 14, 1861. The 68th N. Y. was with the Army of the Potomac, and if the date of March 29 given for Captain Boetticher's capture is accurate, he must have been caught in reconnoitering or skirmishing at the very opening of the Peninsular Campaign, as no regular fight is recorded for the regiment on that day. Captain Boetticher was "dismissed" from the regiment on April 18, 1862—perhaps as missing. His exchange in September has already been noted. He spent a few months at home, and was mustered in again as Captain, Co. B, on February 28, 1863. His discharge came on June 9, 1864, and with it a brevet as lieutenant-colonel for gallant and meritorious conduct.

Boetticher's drawing from nature has been turned into a magnificent color lithograph by our old friends Sarony and Major, now with an additional partner, Joseph F. Knapp. The firm was now increasingly immersed in commercial commission work, and it is therefore not surprising that this print was published by GOUPIL & CO., a New York branch of the Paris house which has always been renowned for superb illustration.

PAGE 99: *Union Prisoners at Salisbury, North Carolina.*

1863.
Drawn from Nature by Act. Major Otto Boetticher.
Published by Goupil & Co.
Lithograph of Sarony, Major & Knapp.
Lithograph, printed in color.
20 3/4 x 37 1/4 inches.

UNION PRISONERS AT SALISBURY, N.C.

The evil name of Libby Prison is second only to that of Andersonville. It had been a tobacco warehouse in Richmond, belonging to the firm of Libby & Son, whose advertisement, obvious in the sketch, says, "Ship chandlers and groceries." Here, in a constant storm of indignation, the commissioned Union officers were held. Conditions were certainly equally bad if not much worse, on hopelessly overcrowded Belle Isle, the island in the James which was the Richmond prison camp for enlisted men, where New York "bounty-jumper" toughs ran wild, but the rank of the inmates of Libby Prison gave greater publicity to their protests. The prison contained eight rooms, 103 by 42 feet each, with unplastered walls, a water-closet—the officers called it a foul privy—on each floor, and a stove to each room. The officers cooked their own food, supplementing the prison fare with purchases of vegetables and fruit; there were bitter and frequent complaints of the rations, which produced official investigations. An acute shortage of supplies, especially meat, in the winter of 1863–64, sent Richmond prices skyhigh, and for a time Libby prisoners received no meat at all. In February 1864 the famous "tunnel escape" was accomplished by 109 officers. Almost half were recaptured, but those who reached Union lines did not understate their sufferings in the prison.

In the fall of 1863 General Lee had protested against holding prisoners in Richmond, and the crowded conditions, lack of guards, and shortage of supplies there had decided General J. H. Winder, inspector-general of prison camps, to remove the prisons farther south. Andersonville, near Macon, Ga., was selected for the new location. Transfer had already begun when, at the end of February came rumors of a Federal cavalry raid under way against Richmond, specifically aiming to free the prisoners. The city was thrown into panic, and the warders placed a charge of powder under Libby Prison, warning that if any attempt were made at escape the warehouse would be blown up. As the raid failed, it could not be proved that the authorities had seriously contemplated such action. However, the prisoners were moved rapidly thereafter to the South, officers to Macon, soldiers to Andersonville, and Libby Prison became only an overnight stop on the trip to a still more fatal place.

By rights, neither WILLIAM C. SCHWARTZBURG of the 24th Wisconsin Volunteers, who drew the sketch, nor John L. Baldwin, 58th Regiment, Indiana Veteran Volunteers, who published it, should have been acquainted with the interior of Libby Prison, which was supposedly reserved for officer guests. Schwartzburg was a private from Milwaukee, mustered in on August 1, 1862, who had been wounded and taken prisoner at Chickamauga. He was eventually mustered out, probably after exchange. He might, being wounded, have been at one of the Richmond hospitals rather than at Belle Isle. John L. Baldwin was from Princeton, Ind., and had been mustered into the 58th Regiment on November 12, 1861. There is no record of his being a prisoner. He served his three years and was mustered out on November 11, 1864.

The photograph of Libby Prison, taken after the surrender of Richmond, shows a curious crowd gathered about the blackly famous building. No doubt some of them are former inmates. The stars and bars, which Schwartzburg saw flying from the roof, are gone, replaced by the victorious Union flag. Miss Josephine Cobb of the National Archives informs us that the photograph was taken from Castle Thunder, in April 1865, by ALEXANDER GARDNER. This Scotchman was brought to America in 1856 by Mathew B. Brady, who valued his experience in the collodion process—the "wet" process which was the first great improvement in photographic technique and supplanted the daguerreotype in the course of the later fifties—and his (then rare) ability to make enlargements. After two years in the New York Studio he was sent, in 1858, to take charge of the new gallery which Brady was opening in Washington. After four years he seceded and opened his own gallery in the capital, but was soon thereafter employed in making maps at the headquarters of the Army of the Potomac. This position on the inside gave Gardner and his son Jim an admirable opportunity for war photography, which was seized, and the result practically incorporated in a two-volume *Sketch Book of the War,* with 50 actual photographs in each volume, published in 1866. This invaluable collection gives the names of many of the Brady and Gardner staff photographers, the men who actually made the negatives. Gardner declared, in his first advertisement of May 26, 1863, that he had "a corps of artists constantly in the field, who are adding to the collection every day." Some 20 years after the war, the Gardner negatives were secured and added to one of the portions of the Brady Collection by its then owners, and it is difficult today to distinguish what is Brady from what is Gardner.

PAGE 102: *Libby Prison, Richmond, Virginia.*

1864.
Sketched
by W. C. Schwartzburg.
Published
by J. L. Baldwin Co.
Lithograph, printed in color.
8 1/2 x 11 3/8 inches.

PAGE 103: *Libby Prison, Richmond, Virginia.*

April 1865.
Photograph
by Alexander Gardner.
9 x 11 inches.

Sketched by W.C. Schwartzburg Co A. 24th Wis. Vol?

LIBBY PRISON, RICHMOND, VA

In December 1863 Capt. Richard B. Winder, a cousin of the harassed commander of Richmond prisons, was sent to the "miserable little hamlet" of Andersonville, near Macon, Ga., to prepare a place for 10,000 prisoners. He encountered considerable opposition in the neighborhood and had to impress labor; supplies were not forthcoming and the prison was in no way ready when the first prisoners arrived on February 27. The 16½ acres (later enlarged to 26) had been enclosed by a stockade of 20-foot pine logs with roofed sentry boxes at intervals. The two gates on the west were protected by a double stockade (shown in the North View, Plate 113). A stream ran through the middle of the yard, and the ground sloping toward it on either side was soon turned into a muddy swamp by thousands of Union feet.

The first comers found no shelter and no bake house. All trees had been cut down and there was no protection from the Georgia sun, welcome enough in February, but soon to become hideously cruel. Lumber needed for barracks was not to be had; the cook house was put by the stream just outside the stockade, where the refuse polluted the water; rations, as more and more prisoners were brought in, grew smaller and smaller—"corn bread and beans," rarely meat. Many arrived sick from the camps to the northward and hospital facilities were hopelessly inadequate. By early May there were 12,000 prisoners in the stockade, and 1,026 had already died.

On March 27, Capt. Henry Wirz, the Swiss-American disciplinarian who had begun as sergeant in charge of prisoners at Tuscaloosa and had been General Winder's assistant in Richmond, came to command the interior of the prison. The only man convicted after the close of the Civil War as a "war criminal," he was tried and hanged in November 1865; and his name has since been synonymous with vindictive cruelty. Reference No. 7 in the "North View" shows "Capt. Wirz taking a prisoner to the stocks." He was accused of the wanton murder of prisoners, of pursuing escaped Yankees with bloodhounds, of personal responsibility for the horrible suffering. Later investigation has shown him to have been an efficient and reasonably well-meaning man, faced with hopeless conditions.

By the end of July there were 31,678 prisoners in the stockade; during the six months from March 1 to August 31, 42,686 cases of disease and wounds were reported. There are 12,912 graves in the National Cemetery—John Burns Walker has printed on the side of the death wagon in his picture, "Dead, 12,877."

JOHN BURNS WALKER was a Pennsylvanian, private in the 141st Regiment, which was recruited in Bradford, Wayne, and Susquehanna Counties in 1862, and mustered in on August 26.

The regiment went first to the defenses of Washington, and then fought at Fredericksburg, Chancellorsville, Gettysburg, and Petersburg. Walker was not with it at the Siege of Petersburg; he had been taken prisoner on May 28, 1864, probably in some of the manoeuvering between Spotsylvania and Cold Harbor, as Grant side-slipped his forces toward Richmond. A strong lad he must have been, well-fortified by Allegheny mountain air, to have stayed alive through those horrible summer months at Andersonville. His release came only at the end of the war, with the General Order of May 26 emptying the Confederate prisons.

Walker had his sketches turned into lithographs by the well-known Philadelphia firm of Sinclair, and we have here a rather late instance of the craftsman who drew the sketch on stone, inserting his name in the plate, a practice which waned with the commercialization of lithography. "Hohenstein," who signed the "North View" and was doubtless also responsible for the "South View" since the style is identical, is in all likelihood the ANTON HOHENSTEIN who drew a handsome portrait of General Lee for Spoliny of Philadelphia in 1867; it is reproduced as Plate 141 in *America on Stone*.

PAGE 106: *Andersonville Prison, Georgia. Representing the imprisonment of 33,000 Union soldiers during the months of June , July and August , 1864.*

1865.
Sketched
by John Burns Walker.
Printed by T. Sinclair.
Tinted lithograph.
14 3/8 x 20 1/8 inches.

PAGE 107: *Andersonville Prison, Georgia.*

1864.
Sketched
by John Burns Walker.
Printed by T. Sinclair.
Tinted lithograph.
14 1/2 x 20 1/8 inches.

ANDERSONVILLE PRISON
GEORGIA.

ANDERSONVILLE PRISON
GEORGIA.

Filed September 25, 1865

At last President Lincoln had found his general. The valiant Army of the Potomac, welded through three years of discipline and drill and up-and-down warfare under changing leadership into a massive and superb fighting instrument, was handed over on March 9, 1864, to Ulysses S. Grant, along with the President's commission as lieutenant general in general command of the Union armies.

Grant lost no time and spared no strength. Since Gettysburg the Union armies in the east had manoeuvred bloodlessly in Northern Virginia, just above the Rappahannock, which had been the southernmost boundary of Federal progress. Richmond, the rebel capital, was still nearly a hundred miles away. On May 4, Grant launched his army across the Rapidan and into the Wilderness. For two days the tangled woods glowed with forest fires, set by the bitter fighting. The result was indecisive, both armies shattered and exhausted. McClellan, Hooker, Pope or Meade would have withdrawn to recuperate: Grant thrust forward to Spotsylvania. Wrote the Confederate, George Cary Eggleston:

"Here was a new Federal general, fresh from the West, and so ill-informed as to the military customs in our part of the country that when the battle of the Wilderness was over, instead of retiring to the north bank of the river and awaiting the development of Lee's plans, he had the temerity to move by his left flank to a new position, there to try conclusions with us again. We were greatly disappointed with General Grant . . ."

Around Spotsylvania the battle raged from May 8 until May 21. Grant wrote to the Chief of Staff, Halleck, on May 11: "We have now ended the sixth day of very hard fighting . . . I propose to fight it out on this line if it takes all summer." Headquarters moved rapidly. Grant's own *Memoirs* describe the stream-filled land:

"The Mattapony River is formed by the junction of the Mat, the Ta, the Po and the Ny rivers, the last being the northernmost of the four. It takes its rise about a mile south and a little east of the Wilderness tavern. The Po rises south-west of the same place, but farther away. Spotsylvania is on the ridge dividing these two streams, and where they are but a few miles apart."

The Telegraph Road, Stanard's Mill, Guiney's Bridge, the Mud Tavern, unknown little local names, figure in the despatches and reports that flew between the field commanders. On May 21, 1864, at 8:25 A. M., Grant sent word to Major General Burnside, Ninth Army Corps, that at 10 his headquarters would be moved to Massaponax Church. By 8:30 the next morning his date line was Guiney's Station, whence he wrote to Halleck, "We now occupy Milford Station and south of the Mattapony on that line." By June 3 he had pushed far south to Cold Harbor, where Lee's army squarely blocked the way on the Richmond road. There three army corps were hurled into the enfilading Confederate fire, and in eight minutes Grant lost most of his 12,000 casualties. The month's campaign, from the Wilderness to Cold Harbor, cost the Union 55,000 soldiers, almost as many as Lee's whole army. But the advance had begun, the smaller Confederate loss could less easily be replaced, and the final grand strategy of the war was being unfolded.

The photographer has caught a moment in the design of this strategy, as Grant and his staff sit studying their maps during the few hours at Massaponax Church. It was perhaps around noon, when the light would be good for a picture. Benches have been brought out of the church for the officers to pose on. The saddled horses are ready—in a few minutes the despatches will be flying. The officer standing at the lower right is not used to being photographed—he moved, and his head is a double blur. Grant himself is lost in thought and does not glance at the camera. Is there a cigar in the side of his mouth?

We have attributed this photograph to Brady, because the negative is in the Brady Collection of the Library of Congress, but there is strong evidence that it was actually taken by Alexander Gardner, or under his auspices. *America in Stone* reproduces as Plate 77 a lithograph drawn and published by C. Inger of Philadelphia which is almost certainly derived from this photograph, and which states that it is "From Small Photograph by Gardner." If this one is representative, the practice of deriving lithographic prints from photographs was aesthetically dismal. In spite of a number of alterations by Inger—most of them decidedly for the worse—the scene is cluttered and inferior in composition. However, Inger was satisfied that Grant did have, or should have had, a cigar in his mouth. The lithograph claims that Sherman, Grant, Hancock, Meade, Garfield, Thomas, Heintzelman, Sickles, and Warren were all present. This was complete nonsense: Sherman and Thomas were fighting the Atlanta campaign; Sickles had not yet returned to active duty after losing a leg at Gettysburg; Heintzelman was in command of one of the northern departments, etc.—another instance of the journalistic abuse of the lithograph.

PAGE 110: *Council of War at Massaponax Church.*

May 21, 1864.
Photograph
by Mathew B. Brady.
6 x 8 inches.

The bloody check at Cold Harbor caused Grant to change his "fight it out on this line" strategy. He abandoned the frontal attack on Richmond, and transferred his whole army south of the James, a notable feat of logistics and engineering. By the 17th of June his armies were in front of Petersburg.

A subsidiary campaign had been planned in that region; the "Army of the James," which had been placed under the command of Gen. Benjamin F. Butler, was to move from its headquarters at Fort Monroe up the James River against Richmond and Petersburg. On May 4 Grant directed Butler to advance. The Army of the James embarked on steamers and sailed toward almost undefended Petersburg. By May 6th Butler was far up the James, and had seized City Point and Bermuda Hundred. In the next week he advanced slowly to Drewry's Bluff. Beauregard, called hurriedly from Charleston to command the Department of North Carolina, which was extended to include Petersburg, resisted Butler with scratch troops, and the political general drew into a strong natural position on a point between the James and the Appomattox Rivers. There he sat, unable to move, while Beauregard gathered together an army from North and South Carolina.

This hermetically sealed spot of Butler's headquarters, Point of Rocks, forms the subject of Waud's drawing. A print from the sketch— wrongly attributed to William Waud—appeared in *Harper's Weekly* on July 23. In the background is identified the *Greyhound,* General Butler's flagship. The date may be any time in late May, June or early July, judging, that is, from the *Harper's* print.

Apparently both Waud brothers visited Butler at his well-placed camp, for it was there that William painted the stirring picture of night signalling. Alfred also sketched the excavating and teamster activities at Dutch Gap Canal. This unfortunate project was an inspiration of General Butler's. During Grant's first attack on Petersburg (June 15–18) a communication was sent to the commander of the Army of the James, in which "the importance of holding a position in advance of his present line [was] urged upon him" (Grant's Report). Butler thought it over, called in the Engineer, Gen. P. S. Michie, and conceived "the idea of cutting a canal through the narrow neck of land, known as Dutch Gap, for the passage of the monitors." On August 10, ground was broken, while Grant's army lay recovering from the terrible repulse of the Crater (July 30). The canal was to be only 174 yards long, but it would cut off 4¾ miles of river navigation. Sixty-seven thousand cubic yards of dirt were excavated. The diggers worked under continuous fire; there were great losses in mules, horses, and carts, and occasional human casualties.

PAGE 112: *Ponton Bridge on the Appomattox, before Petersburg. Point of Rocks. Butlers Headquarters.*

Undated.
Pencil and wash drawing by A. R. Waud.
On gray-tinted paper.
8 3/4 x 13 1/2 inches.

PAGE 113: *Dutch Gap.*

Undated.
Pencil and wash drawing by A. R. Waud.
On green-tinted paper.
6 1/2 x 9 inches.

Pontoon Bridge on the Appomattox near Petersburg,
Point of Rocks. Built by the ... A.R. Waud

Dutch Gap

PAGE 115: *Night Signalling.*

Undated.
Wash drawing
by William Waud.
5 3/4 x 10 1/2 inches.

Harper's Weekly of November 12, 1864, published a print of *Signalling by Torches across James River from General Butler's Headquarters.* An explanation accompanies the picture:

"The messages from the high signal-tower on the other side of the river are read by the sergeant or officer at the telescope, and the reply is signaled by the man with the torch."

It must be seen to be believed, the distressful result of the process which transferred William Waud's fine wash drawing—a high point of his work, as represented in the Library of Congress collection—to the pages of *Harper's.* Every iota of artistic quality has evaporated.

PAGE 117: *Before Petersburg—at Sunrise.*

July 30, 1864.
Pencil and wash drawing
by A. R. Waud.
13 1/2 x 20 inches.

Petersburg, the gateway to Richmond from the South, was confronted by the Union forces in mid-June 1864. General Beauregard, resisting desperately against heavy odds, held off the first attack on June 15–18. Then Lee arrived with the remnants of the Army of Northern Virginia, and Grant and his legions settled down to the siege which was not to be broken till Lee took the final road to Appomattox in the following spring.

The chief event of the long siege was the Battle of the Crater, July 30, 1864. One of Burnside's officers in the Ninth Corps, which held an advanced position in the Union lines, was Lt. Col. Henry Pleasants, a mining engineer from the Pennsylvania coal region. His suggestion that a mine be run under the enemy forts was approved by Burnside, and for a month "the spade took the place of the musket." A 500-foot gallery was run under the lines, with two short lateral galleries. The dirt had to be carried the whole length of the gallery in baskets, and shortage of proper tools slowed the undertaking. But Colonel Pleasants had the mine finished on July 23, and eight magazines of powder were placed in the two side galleries, ready for the explosion.

The mine was exploded before dawn on July 30. "It was a magnificent spectacle, and as the mass of earth went up into the air, carrying with it men, guns, carriages, and timbers, and spread out like an immense cloud as it reached its altitude, so close were the Union lines that the mass appeared as if it would descend immediately upon the troops waiting to make the charge" (Maj. William H. Powell in *Battles and Leaders*). A "crater" 30 feet deep and 170 feet long was left, and through it Burnside's men attacked, in a hopeless confusion of débris. The furious Southerners, fighting at the peak of their magnificent courage, flung them back. The whole operation cost almost 4,000 Union men—"a stupendous failure," Grant said.

Powell's "magnificent spectacle" is the subject of Alfred Waud's fine drawing, in which the staff, well back on high breastworks, watches the explosion as it occurs. The mouth of the mine gallery is evident behind a small clump of trees at the right. The towers of Petersburg stand out in the distance.

Before Petersburg at Sunrise

A.R. Waud

118

PAGE 119: *Sheridan's
Wagon Trains in the
Valley–Early morning.*

Undated.
Pencil and wash drawing
by A. R. Waud.
On light brown paper.
6 3/4 x 19 1/4 inches.

While Grant and the main force of the Army of the Potomac lay facing Lee's worn veterans at Petersburg, diversionary activities raged in western Virginia. The brilliant Confederate cavalry general, "Jeb" Stuart, was dead—killed at Yellow Tavern, six miles north of Richmond, which he had saved from the raid (May 9–24, 1864) of three divisions of Northern cavalry, 10,000 strong, under its new commander, Maj. Gen. Philip Sheridan. But Lee's able infantry general, Jubal A. Early, was moving in the Shenandoah Valley. Lee had detached him from the main force to drive away a small Union division near Lynchburg, and Early turned in a bold and dangerous move northeastward. Washington was again in panic as Lew Wallace with a ragtag force delayed but did not stop Early at the Monocacy (July 9). Lincoln wired to Grant for aid, and, to Baltimore citizens, "Let us be vigilant but keep cool." While inspecting the Washington defenses, the President was sworn at and unceremoniously ordered out of danger by a young lieutenant from Massachusetts, named Oliver Wendell Holmes, Jr. Then Grant sent troops, Early retreated behind the Blue Ridge, and Washington recovered from its "terrible fright."

Sheridan and his cavalry now moved against Early in the Shenandoah Valley. Their orders were to devastate. There were quick movements, skirmishes, battles. On September 19 the armies clashed near Winchester. Sheridan had been in Washington, consulting with the General Staff; on his return he heard the firing "twenty miles away," and rode post-haste to snatch victory out of what looked like disaster.

Then Sheridan turned to his second task. Alfred Waud's picture shows the early morning movement of the procession of wagon trains. Nothing that could be of use to the army was left behind them.

*In the Shenandoah Valley, the millwheels rot.
(Sheridan has been there.) Where the houses stood,
Strong houses, built for weather, lasting it out,
The chimneys stand alone. The chimneys are blackened.
(Sheridan has been there.) This Valley has been
The granary of Lee's army for years and years.
Sheridan makes his report on his finished work.
"If a crow intends to fly over the Valley now
He'll have to carry his own provisions," says Sheridan.*
(S. V. Benét, *John Brown's Body*.)

PAGE 121: *Bombardment of Fort Fisher, January 15, 1865.*

From a drawing by T. F. Laycock. Published by Endicott & Co. Lithograph. printed in color. 6 x 17 1/2 inches.

The reduction of Fort Fisher was the final large-scale naval action of the war. This strong coastal defense stood at the entrance to the Cape Fear River before Wilmington, N. C., guarding that last remaining harbor of the blockade-runners bringing supplies from overseas. Lee had written from Petersburg in the winter of 1864 that Fort Fisher must be held at all costs. Gens. B. F. Butler and Godfrey Weitzel, in combination with Admiral Porter's 60-ship squadron had tried to take it in December 1864, but the stout North Carolina garrison held out behind their powerful works.

In January 1865 a second expedition was sent out. On the 13th, 8,000 Union troops under Gen. Alfred H. Terry were landed on the beach to the north. Porter's armada (with 600 heavy guns, according to Gen. Braxton Bragg, the commander of the Confederate forces in Wilmington, who failed to support the fort) attacked from the sea. The bombardment went on for three days, the five monitors keeping up a fitful fire all night. The guns of the fort were silenced on the 14th. On that day, relates Col. William Lamb, the Confederate commander, a "stupid" flat-bottomed steam transport, loaded with stores for Lee's army, sailed right into the enemy's fleet and, of course, fell an easy captive.

On January 15th the full bombardment reopened at 9 a. m. At noon a landing detachment of sailors and marines, about 2,000 men from 35 ships, were sent ashore. At the angle of the two faces of the fort they were caught in an intense rifle fire from the ramparts. There were many casualties, and the mixed force retreated in "a disorderly rout" (Lamb). Meanwhile the troops under Terry had approached and gained the highest parapets to the north. The way was cleared before them by renewed heavy fire from the monitors. The iron-clad vessels can be seen to the right behind the line of larger ships in Laycock's print.

Of T. F. LAYCOCK, the sailor artist who dedicated his picture to his commanding officer, nothing is known beyond his record in Callahan's *List of Officers:*

Laycock, Thomas F. Mate, 26 January, 1863. Acting Ensign, 7 April, 1864. Acting Master, 20 March, 1865. Honorably discharged 2 December, 1865.

The officer honored by his obedient servant was Commodore Sylvanus W. Godon, an officer of the old Navy, who had started his career as a midshipman in 1819. In 1855 he was a commander, in 1862 a captain, commanding the sloop *Mohican*. He was promoted to commodore on January 2, 1863. In 1866 he was named Rear Admiral, and retired with that rank in 1871. The lithograph, from the great house of Endicott, is a handsome piece of work.

BOMBARDMENT OF FORT FISHER

The famous march to the sea began on November 16, 1864. General Sherman, commanding the Military Division of the Mississippi, had the day before burned Atlanta, ending the long summer campaign against Joe Johnston and Hood. His army consisted of 55,329 infantry, 5,063 cavalry, 1,812 artillery, an aggregate of 62,204 officers and men. They marched out of the city smouldering in ruins by the Decatur road, singing "John Brown's body lies a-mouldering in the grave, His soul goes marching on."

Their purpose was the destruction of supplies, and the sixty-mile-wide course through Georgia was to the Union soldiers a picnic procession. Field orders specified that the order of march should be as nearly as possible by four parallel roads, that "the army will forage liberally on the country during the march," that foraging parties, "under the command of one or more discreet officers," were to gather and keep in the wagons 10 days' provisions and three days' forage. "To corps commanders alone is intrusted the power to destroy mills, houses, cotton-gins etc.; . . . should the inhabitants . . . manifest local hostility, then army commanders should order and enforce a devastation more or less relentless . . ." Horses, mules and wagons might be appropriated "freely and without limit," though with discrimination in favor of the "poor and industrious, usually neutral or friendly." The troops were ordered to "refrain from abusive or threatening language."

The right wing of the army, under Gen. O. O. Howard, met some slight resistance near Macon, but Sherman and his staff marched unopposed into the State capital, Milledgeville, on the 23d. The State officials had fled, and the officers "(in the spirit of mischief) gathered together in the vacant hall of Representatives, elected a Speaker, and constituted themselves the Legislature of the State of Georgia." Sherman "was not present at these frolics, but heard of them at the time, and enjoyed the joke." Farther on, at the Oconee, there was feeble resistance, soon broken. The march went on, through Waynesboro and Millen, and on December 10 Sherman invested the city of Savannah. On the 13th Fort McAllister, the main defense on the Ogeechee River guarding the approach by sea, was captured. After a 10-day siege the Confederate defenders fled across the Savannah River into South Carolina, and Sherman estimated that damage in Georgia had amounted to $100,000,000—most of it "simple waste and destruction."

The general stayed in Savannah until January 21, 1865, when he started his troops northward for a campaign in South Carolina. It was during these first three weeks of the last year of the war that William Waud sketched Sherman reviewing his troops. The picture was reproduced in *Harper's Weekly* of February 11, with an additional section at the right in which are shown the heads and shoulders of marching infantry.

PAGE 125: *The Last of General Lee's Headquarters, Petersburg– after the battle.*

Pencil drawing
by A. R. Waud.
On light green paper.
Undated.
6 1/2 x 9 inches.

On April 3, 1865, after more than eight months of siege, the Union army marched into abandoned Petersburg, a ruined city of the dead. The desolation of defeat breathes heavily through Waud's tragic drawing, in which the four chimneys of the house rise starkly from shattered walls, and the very débris takes on the shape of hooded mourners.

The ruins of Genl. Lees Headquarters. Petersburg - after the battle

PAGE 127: *Grand Review of the Army, at Washington.*

May 1865.
Photograph
by Mathew B. Brady.
8 x 10 inches.

On the Capitol of the United States the flag flies at half mast, the windows and pillars are bound with crape. The joy of victory, the happiness of welcoming home brave soldiers, is shadowed by the cruel sense of loss. Not only will half a million men who lie in the Southland never again come home; Lincoln, leader and symbol, is barely a month in his grave, and many spectators of the Victory Parade are still dressed in mourning black. The trial of the assassins, Paine, Atzerodt, Herold, Mrs. Surratt and the rest, has been suspended during the grand review of the armies.

On May 23 the spectators gathered. The reviewing stand for President, Cabinet and General Grant was in front of the White House, but the crowds lined the streets solidly from the Capitol the length of Pennsylvania Avenue. All day the veterans of the Army of the Potomac rode and marched by. The next day too, from early morning to late afternoon, the armies paraded. By nightfall 150,000 veterans had passed the reviewing stand.

Brady's photograph shows a tiny section of the spectators. Congressmen with their wives, daughters and parasols, sit and stand before the Capitol where, as in 1945, the bands, the floats, and the machines of war gather for the formation of the parade. The dome has been finished during these four long years of war, and though she cannot be seen in this picture, the nation knows that helmeted Freedom rests victorious on her sheathed sword.